RUSSIAN ROULETTE

RUSSIAN ROULETTE

Afghanistan Through Russian Eyes

Gennady Bocharov

Translated from the Russian by Alyona Kojevnikov

 A Cornelia & Michael Bessie Book
An Imprint of HarperCollins*Publishers*

FIRST EDITION

Designed by Alma Orenstein

Library of Congress Cataloging-in-Publication Data

Bocharov, Gennadiĭ Nikolaevich.
  Russian roulette: Afghanistan through Russian eyes /
Gennady Bocharov. —1st ed.
    p. cm.
  "A Cornelia & Michael Bessie book."
  ISBN 0-06-039110-3
    1. Afghanistan—History—Soviet occupation, 1979–1989—
Personal narratives, Soviet.—2. Bocharov, Gennadiĭ Nikolae-
vich—Journeys—Afghanistan.—3. Journalists—Soviet Union—
Biography. I. Title.
DS371.2.B62—1990
958.104′5—dc20   89-46074

90 91 92 93 94 CG/HC 10 9 8 7 6 5 4 3 2 1

The Journalist's Story

And I turned myself to behold wisdom, and madness, and folly: for what can the man do that cometh after the king? even that which hath already been done.

ECCLESIASTES 2:12

I ARRIVED IN KABUL on 14 February 1980. Dirty snow blanketed the city. Tanks and armored personnel carriers (APCs) stood at every crossroads. Shivering soldiers of the "limited contingent of Soviet forces" perched on the vehicles, the collars of their battle jackets raised, trying to warm themselves by smoking as they reckoned up the time they had spent in Afghanistan.

It came to six weeks.

I had been booked into the Kabul Hotel, right in the center of the Afghan capital. The telephone cord in Room 117, my temporary home, had been ripped out of the wall. A glass lamp shade hung askew under the high ceiling. The door and walls of the room were riddled by hundreds of bullets.

That room reminded one forcibly of a site of battle.

For two days no hotel staff came anywhere near me, nor was my room cleaned. If they encountered me in the corridors, they merely looked at me in a very meaningful way.

Room 117 was where the U.S. ambassador, Adolf Dubbs, had been ruthlessly killed. Since his murder, the room had remained untenanted.

I was the first. As Fate willed it, I was to experience the worst night of my life right there. But that was still to come. At the moment, I wanted, more than anything, to find out what had happened to the ill-starred ambassador. It was not really out of ordinary human compassion:

3

the dead have no need of it, anyway. I was motivated, first and foremost, by a purely professional, journalistic interest:

- Why had Dubbs left his car?
- Why had he agreed to talk to strangers?
- Why did he end up in the hotel?

I didn't learn much. The ambassador had been stopped by four men dressed in traffic policemen's uniforms. He had been dragged out of the car by force and hustled into the hotel at gunpoint. His captors then barricaded themselves into Room 117, and demanded the release of a Shia Muslim leader, Bakhruddin Bakhez, from prison. Sometime later, Dubbs was mortally wounded.

An assault was mounted on Room 117: three of the terrorists were killed, and the fourth wounded. He could have clarified everything, but he, too, was dead some five minutes later. He was not killed in Room 117, but in the hotel lobby. A man leapt out at him from behind a large cutout cardboard advertisement of an Air France stewardess to the left of the porter's office, and stabbed him with a knife. His mission accomplished, the unidentified assassin disappeared. He sprinted through a side door into a courtyard with three immense Himalayan cedars, never to be seen again. Trying to catch him would have been a hopeless task. Almost certainly he vanished into the warrens of the city, where anyone at all could get lost, and then headed for the countryside—where everyone got lost.

Dubbs died on arrival at his embassy. My attempts to get at the truth proved fruitless.

The killing of the ambassador was overtaken by other killings. New tragedies and new events drove it into the background. The new history of the country was born on 26 December 1979, on that thunderous day when Kabul airport saw the landings of 215 planes with red stars on their fuselages.

Room 117 in Kabul Hotel, where I was destined to live, was on the first floor. Its only window, crisscrossed with sturdy wire mesh, faced the People's House. A huge red flag waved above the crenellated walls and towers of this former residence of Afghanistan's rulers. It replaced the discarded green banner.

It was from here that Babrak Karmal ruled in place of the slain Amin. There was not a single Afghan among the guards of the first secretary of the Central Committee of the People's Democratic Party of Afghanistan (PDPA). Soviet paratroopers were also the guards of the People's House. Soviet and Afghan army tanks and APCs stood at the stone gates. I could see them from my window. I could not help remembering how many times I had seen similar sights in different parts of the world, and how quickly heavy armor becomes evidence of the impotence of an enforced regime.

Late in the evening on my day of arrival I was received by the Soviet ambassador in Afghanistan, Tabeyev.

He had succeeded Puzanov, who had simply slept through the April coup, which was shortly to be hailed as the "April revolution." It's my guess that he heard about the coup from Moscow. And Moscow itself learned of the coup by radio.

Like his predecessor Puzanov, Tabeyev was not a career diplomat. He had been sent to Kabul from the post of first secretary of a provincial regional party committee.

I spent less than fifteen minutes with him. The future deputy chairman of the Presidium of the Russian federation was patently exhausted. He sat under the flickering light of an overhead lamp and listened to reports from his advisers. A large portrait of Brezhnev graced the wall behind him. Tabeyev's relations with the general secretary were well known here.

A constant stream of people passed through the ambassador's study. Party advisers reported on the heels of their military colleagues, to be replaced by the KGB; these, in turn, were pressed by Soviet Ministry of the Interior officials, by economic, transport, and other advisers, and by diplomats.

Those February days of 1980 were the crucible of the majority of the tragedies of the new history of Afghanistan. The tightest knots of Afghan politics began to draw in. Dead ends, from which no way out was ever found, appeared and multiplied.

The ambassador listened to everyone in silence. Information on casualties among Soviet soldiers, terrorism, the situation in Kabul, and in the country in general did not alter the expression on his face. Unrelieved exhaustion rendered it dark and immobile.

"Very good," he said to me, hardly realizing that neither he nor I had, in fact, exchanged even a few words of any significance. "Very good," he repeated, and extended his hand in dismissal.

It was almost like a benediction.

A charge of dynamite wrecked a whole wall of Kabul's central post office. A Czech, who had been mistaken for a Soviet citizen, was killed in a four-story department store not far from my hotel. A group of Soviet sappers was seized and brutally savaged. The mutilation of their corpses made the blood run cold. A military transport plane crashed in Kabul airport under unclarified circumstances, killing all the paratroopers on board.

Every such instance, taken by itself, remained an isolated occurrence. But their sum amounted to war.

Soon, this became obvious to all.

Quite a large number of the diplomats and advisers knew everything. But nobody talked of it officially. Any discussions of "dangerous" matters with the resident members of the Central Committee of the Communist Party of the Soviet Union were also out of the question. I suspected that there was no trust between them, either. Rather, they preferred not to discuss real situations, but to engage in wishful thinking.

Rumors have been an intrinsic feature of everyday life in eastern cities from times immemorial. They had also become an integral part of life in communist Moscow. Both these norms—the eastern and the communist—fused in Kabul, reinforcing each other and producing a mind-boggling result: total veracity. Everything that was rumored in those days came true in time. Not a single item of disinformation! I know of no other such situation in history.

It was said that by the time Babrak Karmal landed in Kabul in a Soviet plane, there were more than twenty thousand Soviet soldiers and officers in Afghanistan. It was said that Babrak's radio address to the Afghan nation was written with the assistance of representatives of a foreign power. It was further said that Babrak Karmal—or, as he was soon to become known for convenience, "Boris Karlovich"—did not ask the Soviets for military assistance. It was hinted that Ogarkov (the former chief of staff of the armed forces of the USSR) was categorically opposed to the intervention. All Kabul maintained that Amin's henchmen had suffocated Taraki* with a pillow, and killed his wife for good measure. Everyone was convinced that Amin, denounced as a CIA agent, had been killed by Soviet paratroopers in the Darulaman palace. There were those who maintained that a Soviet medical corps colonel and a nurse who were attending Amin were killed with him. It was bruited around that during a battle with the guards, Soviet paratroopers shot up, at point-blank range, a relief group of their own in an APC.

I talked to the soldiers. They were all alert, ready for action; they bore themselves well and with patriotic fervor. "We are here at the request of the legal government," they would assure me, a journalist, even though no such question had been put to them. Some said that they were in Afghanistan of their own free will. There were those who proudly declaimed a military secret known only to them and their immediate superiors: they had beaten the Americans into Afghanistan by a mere two to four days, maybe even by a few hours. How about that?!

---

*Taraki was one of the puppet presidents of Afghanistan and headed the PDPA.

"Everything's fine," said the soldiers. Only one of them said: "We live like animals. We haven't been able to wash even once. There's no firewood, so we freeze. And the food's hardly fit for pigs. Some of us already have body lice."

The day before my night of terror was overcast and cold. The fog seemed impenetrable. Surly, silent people trudged through the deepening dusk along dirty, wet pavements, which were never cleared of snow. The usually raucous street loudspeakers, which normally churned out a continuous stream of wailing eastern music, were silent. The shops and stalls along the main shopping street, the Maivande, had closed surprisingly early.

Five armed young Afghans—members of the divisions defending the revolution—sat in the hotel lobby. The hotel was under guard around the clock. I went up to the first floor, and looked out onto the square through the large plate-glass windows. The far end of the square, where there was a mosque and a cinema, could not be seen for fog. However, the near end, where there was a fence draped with clothing for sale, was clearly visible. Vendors were hurriedly pulling down cotton vests and faded shirts, stuffing them away in bags. Clearly, something was afoot. As everywhere else in the streets, there was a growing crowd of grim, threatening people. From time to time they would look around and confer among themselves.

I went to my room.

Darkness came quickly. A dull, strange sound swelled outside. Only a very large crowd could generate such a noise. I would go up to my window to peer out, but the streetlights were off and everything was dark.

Then came a burst of machine-gun fire—they were shooting at the main entrance of the hotel. There was no return fire. The noise of the crowd rose.

Someone hammered loudly on my door.

"The hell with it!" I decided. "You'll have to break in!"

"Open up!" shouted a familiar voice. "Come on, hurry!"

A colleague from *Pravda* barged into the room. There was blood on his face, and his hands shook uncontrollably.

"The fucking bastards!" he bellowed, "they've busted up my car! They bashed in the hood with sticks!"

"They busted your head, too," I pointed out.

"Fuck that! There's hundreds of them out there. The guards in the lobby have run for it. Those bastards out there want blood. There's hundreds of them out in the streets, I tell you! Where's the phone?"

"Disappeared with Dubbs."

He didn't understand what I was talking about.

"We should all stick together. Quickly, let's join the others!"

There were not more than twenty people in the huge, unfriendly Kabul Hotel. Only Soviet citizens. Apart from some TASS, *Izvestiya*, and *Literaturnaya Gazeta* reporters, there were diplomats from the Ministry of Foreign Affairs of the USSR, Party Central Committee officials, and the pilots of two military transport planes that were at the service of high-ranking army commanders. For camouflage, these pilots wore "Aeroflot" uniforms.

We went up to the second floor. The others, alarmed by the noise and the rising tension, had left their rooms and gathered near a corner alcove beside a tall, dusty standard lamp. I went over to the dark blue drapes and opened them a chink. This window faced in the opposite direction from the window in my room. The sight that met my eyes was truly dreadful. The neighboring "Pak" hotel was already ablaze like a haystack. Two overturned Chavdar buses—a gift from fraternal Bulgaria to the people of revolutionary Afghanistan—smoldered in the middle of the road. The flames cast an eerie glow over a multitude of turbaned men and veiled women.

"Allah akbar! Allah akbar!" roared the throng. "Shuravi—marg, marg, marg!"—"Allah is great! Death to the Soviets—death, death, death!"

The hotel was completely surrounded by the Islamic faithful. Thick smoke from the street penetrated into the hotel and drifted up the stairs and down the wide, empty corridor.

The telephone lines had been cut. We had one walkie-talkie, which wouldn't work no matter what we did to it.

The Soviet commandant of Kabul was among those present. But what could he do? Whom could we call?

The situation seemed hopeless. I did not consider myself a novice in such situations. I had seen a lot in Vietnam, in Laos, in Bangladesh, in Angola. But that was one thing, and the present situation was something completely different.

We had one grenade. Just one between all of us. But who could say how things would turn out? There is not one atheist under the sun who can predict what will happen in the next minute in the world of believers. Nor a single Christian who can foretell what will occur in the next moment in the world of the Muslims. No believer wants to know a world other than his own.

One grenade for all of us—what plenty!

"Allah akbar! Shuravi—marg, marg, marg!"

Each of us knew that the fanatics take their time about killing you. We knew that the first thing they do is pierce your forearms with knives. Then they hack off your ears, your fingers, your genitals, put out your eyes, and slit your nostrils. Even after death, the victim is not allowed to rest: they will go on slashing, cutting, severing, until even the death of the infidel is desecrated.

Just one grenade! We heard the nearby yells, breathed the smoke of nearby fires, and prayed to Fate to grant us instant death. But who could be sure of that? One grenade was not enough to kill us all outright.

I stared at the worn patterns on the carpet underfoot. I feared the knives in the hands of my medieval contemporaries. But just as much as those knives I feared dishonor. I found myself shivering convulsively, uncontrollably.

Even silence was incredibly difficult. I assumed that I was ready, if not for everything, then at least for much. It seemed to me that I was sufficiently experienced in handling complex, dangerous situations. I trusted my memory. I had long ago reached the conclusion that memory is not just man's friend or enemy, or a stimulus to consciousness. Memory is the storehouse of experience. And if there is something that can be relied on, it is your own experience. There are times when personal experience serves a man better than the collective experience of humanity. I had often noted that in the external, superficial layer of memory not everything is stable, not everything is explicable. But memory has depth. And that is the crucial thing. All that has ever occurred in your life, that which has already been overcome and experienced, is processed in a very specific way by in-depth memory. It is processed and then filed away in the storehouse of experience. And it is from this that you draw virtually everything. And most importantly, strength to fight.

Yet here my experience proved useless. Worthless. You cannot fight destiny. You are powerless. And the form of death facing you is much more terrifying than Death itself.

No matter how hard I clenched my teeth, they chattered as though I had been linked up to some infernal vibrator.

Just think of it—I was afraid of a confrontation with Islam. With Islamic fanaticism. Yet all it was, when all was said and done, was just another form of human belief, no more.

No more.

No more.

No more.

Possibly I was not the only one to experience such shameful fear that night—maybe we all did. I don't know, I didn't see. I tried to get a grip on myself. I even went over to the window again. The crowd battered on the walls of the hotel.

"Allah akbar! Allah akbar!"

I had missed my best chance in the "Bermuda triangle." One moment, and it could have all been over. How beautifully the airplane's engines had burned. How hopelessly the Boeing had come in for a landing at Barranquil. How magnificently it might have impacted! But

I survived there, to die here. And to die like this.

How absurd.

How unfair.

How inevitable.

The smell of burning became stifling, like felt. One of the Central Committee officials assumed leadership. He was pale, businesslike, and controlled. "Keep together," he repeated. "Nobody move so much as a step. We won't be abandoned. Rescue must already be under way."

And in fact there were sounds of gunfire outside. But who was doing the shooting? The sounds of a piano drifted out through the open door of a nearby room—someone had left a transistor radio switched on. The music seemed to turn reality into an absurdity, and acted as an anchor to sanity.

The shooting grew louder. Then came the sound of running feet.

"This is it," I thought simply.

But it was our boys! Paratroopers, boiling with fury and armed to the teeth. They raced along the wide, smoke-filled corridor, and a young, bowlegged major kept calling out, like an automaton:

"Rebellion! Rebellion! Rebellion! Everyone into the APCs! Get moving!"

Since that moment, I have known that if you have so much as a minute, then you still have a future.

I was shoved into the third APC. Somebody's heavy boot ground into my left cheek. My right cheek was pressed against the ice-cold viewscope, through which I could see, with one eye, the night's doings in risen Kabul: fires burned, showing turbulent crowds, mud-brick shops, mosques—and the last of them, the Mahommed Yakub-khan.

My Afghan war began on that February night in 1980. I spent the rest of the night on a cold table in one of the offices of the Soviet embassy. Having returned from the Muslim year of 1358 into my own Christian 1980, I experienced nothing. All I felt was sore muscles.

Only sore muscles.

Time does not flow laterally, like a river; time flows vertically, from bottom to top, raising all the murk, all the dirt, and all evil from the depths. And carrying it from epoch to epoch. It shall always be so. While there are depths and heights.

A Soldier's Tale

... HUNDREDS OF UNCONTROLLED reactive rockets rained down on them from low-flying helicopters, great fountains of earth and stones shot up to obscure the sky. The earth groaned, and in its groans, gave birth to corpses.

◄   ◄   ◄

They drained fuel from the engines and then, God help us, poured it over them and set them alight.

The wind was quite brisk, but it could not disperse the acrid smoke. Everyone breathed with difficulty and cursed. And then there was that damned "spook" who'd been shot through the pelvis, lying there on the lip of the ravine like a ghost, exacerbating already frayed nerves.

He'd been hit just as he'd frozen into immobility, thinking, no doubt, that he'd managed to save his skin. But he was wrong—and that's when they got him.

Of course, they buried him later. Out with the sappers' spades, chunk-clink, under the stones of Registan, and that was that. He's human, after all, said the sergeant. No matter what.

But they burned the camels. Spilled fuel over them and set them on fire. The camels were dead by then, anyway. They'd been brought down earlier by Kalashnikov machine-gun fire.

Who had done the shooting? Why—everyone. It was combat, after all.

The caravan they'd seized didn't yield much: just some small arms and a couple of dismantled ground-to-air rocket launchers. Not a rich haul. Not like the day before yesterday, when the boys had brought down seventeen "humpbacks" in one attack. All credit was due to the sergeant for that: he'd fired at one of the camels in the middle, and the whole caravan blew sky-high. Seventeen camels loaded with explosives flew into the air simultaneously. There were still buzzards circling above the ravine: a feast for them, and a celebration for the squad.

But this second lot was nothing to get excited about. However, that was a relative judgment: it was small beer for the more experienced, but it was hell for the new boys.

Everyone was hungry and set out their rations on the ground. They sat in the shadow of the Mi-8 helicopter, chewing, laughing, and swearing. But he couldn't bring himself to join their circle, and wandered around aimlessly. He couldn't even think of eating. He felt the bile rising to his throat—this was awful, awful, the camels hadn't even stopped burning yet. Three of them lay nearby, giving out a vile, stomach-turning stench.

He'd seen camels in the zoo in Moscow. During his school holidays. On a class excursion. As soon as they arrived in Moscow, they went to Krasnaya Presnya, to the zoo. Why don't we go to Red Square, to the Kremlin? he asked his teacher. I don't like to see animals in cages!

Because the Red Square is always open, explained the teacher, and the zoo closes tomorrow for sanitary measures. The camels in the zoo were not in cages, of course, but in fenced-off enclosures. One of them, he recalled, looked at him out of sleepy eyes. Looked at him, and then spat. Sticky saliva trickled down his face and shirt. Why did you do that? he yelled at the camel, affronted. Did I do you any harm?!

The time had come to take revenge for that spit. A long way from Moscow, indeed. And anyway, it was not he who took vengeance; the shooting and burning was done by the others. He'd just loosed off a shot for the sake of form.

Heat. Nausea.

He avoided looking in the direction where the dead spook was being buried. They'd folded him in half, like a big rag doll. Instead, he turned away and stared at the rotors of the Mi-8. As though he didn't know.

It was all too much to take.

That night he had had his first taste of combat. Even though the caravan was pretty poor, it was their legitimate target. But something more serious had occurred: he had remained alive. Nobody else remarked on this, but he knew that he might have died, yet stayed alive. He did not yet know his fate, and when this happened he could barely believe it.

They had prepared an ambush. They were waiting for the appearance of the caravan, the remains of which burned nearby now. There was no lessening of the heat even at night. He had not expected such temperatures in Afghanistan.

They lay facing the track, a gentle slope at their backs. The squad had been split up into two groups. The track wound from afar, and was the only possible route for the caravan to take. Strange, foreign names echoed in his head—Miram-Shakhet, Chirat, Djobe, Quetti—the captain said that it was from those places that arms were brought into this zone.

He lay at the highest turning of the track, while the majority of the soldiers were down below, near the floor of the ravine.

When he saw the shadow of his own head, he realized that something had happened down there. Twisting around, he saw the glare of flares. At the same moment, there was a chattering of machine guns and automatic rifles. The fighting had started below.

He pressed his belly flat to the ground, clutching his sniper's rifle (he was still a scout), and, his heart hammering, strained his ears to hear the bursting of hand grenades and the frenzied roaring of injured camels. Fear pressed at his temples like a leaden band, drove the air out of his lungs. At that moment he remembered what the more experienced hands called "a greeting"—that is, a greeting from death. You get it when you least expect it, they said. To explain it fully was impossible.

Senses at breaking point, quivering like a driven dog, he suddenly became aware of imminent death. And tried to burrow even deeper into the ground.

Someone was about to kill him. He shot a glance to the right, where the captain lay, illuminated by the light of the flares. He lay perfectly still, as though oblivious to the sounds of conflict below.

But *he* could hear, and looking around—see.

He knew with sudden certainty that something had to be changed. So he changed his position. Propping himself up on his elbows, he edged over toward the captain.

And at that very moment, a bullet whined past his ear and buried itself in the ground. Just where his head had been a second ago.

A greeting from Death.

He didn't even flinch. He was so engrossed in the picture of battle that he didn't even shudder. The feeling of mortal danger penetrated his consciousness for a fleeting moment, and was swallowed up by the general overriding fear.

He cast a look around, eyes straining—but there was no running figure to be seen. Nothing stirred between him and those who fought below. It must have been a ricochet bullet.

"The ravine!" shouted the captain suddenly. "Face the ravine!"

Rolling over, he pointed his rifle in the direction of the ravine. Bursts of fire grew louder and louder. The captain's walkie-talkie crackled: the group commander was ordering them to move left, over to where the caravan was being driven.

But the captain seemed in no hurry. So then he came to a decision: reaching out his hand, he found a little hole in the ground and poked around for the bullet. But the stony soil was hard as granite. No chance. Anyway, what do I want with it? he thought briefly. It's not mine any longer. In the next moment they were on their feet, running toward the second turning in the trail, toward the remnants of the caravan. The camels, maddened by fear, galloped wildly. Two spooks ran beside them, seeking cover behind the animals' huge, heaving bellies.

"Shoot at their legs, their legs!" yelled someone out

of the rocket-illuminated yellow murk of swirling dust. "Get their legs!"

A spray of bullets punctured the camels' bellies and brought them to the ground, clumsily, onto their forelegs, roaring with pain. One camel flipped over completely and skidded along the sand on its hump and the boxes strapped to it. The spooks, robbed of cover, sprinted in different directions. One escaped, but they got the other one. Bullets raked through his pelvis just as he got to the lip of the ravine.

The remains of the camels smoldered and stank, the eaters around the Mi-8 talked noisily, and he kept pacing the hard sand. He wondered at how easily and quickly they had all adapted to a new and frightening existence, and lived this life to the exclusion of all else.

From that night on, he was one of them.

When the rotors of the helicopter started spinning, the captain gave him a little shove toward the metal ladder, and said amiably: "Off we go. The main thing is we had no casualties."

◀   ◀   ◀

The school Nikolai Ivanov attended was the best in Zagorsk. By the time he was called to the local recruiting office, thirteen of his local contemporaries had already gone to Afghanistan. Two had returned almost immediately—in zinc coffins. A third came back later—without hands.

Those were bad days.

The other lads of the same age were scared, even though they concealed their fear and exchanged meaningful glances at meetings in an attempt at bravado. When they parted at the gates of their homes they would ask, carelessly: "Well? Off to 'Afghan,' eh?"

Their parents were frankly alarmed.

There was particular indignation in the town when the local authorities prohibited any mention of the place of death on the tombstones: not a word about Afghanistan! All you can put on them, they told the bereaved parents, is the name of the deceased and the date. That's it.

"Did my son die in a drunken brawl?" wept the mother of one of the dead boys, complaining to her neighbors. "Or did he smash himself up on a motorbike? He's an 'internationalist,' isn't he?"

In time, the people of Zagorsk found out that this directive was not something thought up by their local authorities. The prohibition applied everywhere, to the graves of all the "Afghans," wherever they were buried.

There was nothing to be done. Nobody could gather up the courage to defy the directive.

There were young men in Zagorsk who were very keen to go to Afghanistan. Nikolai knew them. One of them was the son of a military man who spent most of his time somewhere in the north of the country. Another was the son of an alcoholic. A third was the son of the secretary of the regional party organization.

This particular lad had declared his intention to go to Afghanistan in the ninth grade. His father was aghast.

"But you keep urging us at meetings to become 'internationalists,'" protested the son with righteous indignation. "Don't you?"

"Yes!" shouted his father, "but that's in general

terms! That's a slogan! But you are my only son, and that's reality! Nobody says you can't be an internationalist! Go ahead! But here. *Here!*"

The son would smile, and go off to meet his friends. In their company, he was more open. "In 'Afghan,' " he would say, "I'll get a machine gun. And then I'll make tracks for the West—through Pakistan. It's been done before—I heard about such escapes on the Voice of America. There's no way I'd be able to do that from Zagorsk!"

Nikolai was conscripted in the spring. He served six months in Central Asia, was twice in Tashkent, and even saw Samarkand.

His military service proceeded normally. He decided that he was not made of the stuff needed in Afghanistan. Then everything changed in a single day: hurried preparations, embarkation, and a flight into the unknown in a military plane.

After half an hour of flight over the Pamir range, a corporal sitting beside Nikolai peered out and said that there was nothing to choose between the Pamirs and the Hindu Kush. "We're flying over the Hindu Kush," he added. And an hour later, the plane really did land in Kabul.

Nikolai sent his first letter home to Zagorsk only a week after arrival.

"I'm doing my duty," he wrote, "everything is the same as before." But then, forgetting himself for a moment, he added: "Never in my life have I seen such dirty and tattered people. Many of them are like ghosts. But they are people, and some of them even drive around in cars. However, the majority push handcarts of wood around Kabul. I feel very sorry for them."

Nikolai was an honest and openhearted young man. Fair-haired, striking gray eyes, a classically oval face. He enjoyed considerable success among the girls. One of them had tried to entice him into her bed while they were still at school. He panicked and held back, but then regretted it bitterly. When his friends boasted about their romantic conquests he would cite this incident, pretending that he had gone all the way.

After graduating from high school and before being called up by the army, Nikolai got a driver's license. His father worked as a truck driver, earning a living behind the steering wheels of huge, heavy Maz lorries. So it was natural for Nikolai to learn to drive. His mother worked in the same sphere, too, as a controller at the local motor depot. She was a frail, delicate creature who looked more like a schoolgirl than a mother of a grown-up son. In those far-off days—almost seven months ago!—when Nikolai was still at home, they were frequently mistaken for a young man out with his girl, or even for a brother and sister.

In Afghanistan, Nikolai served in Intelligence, but only for the first two months. After that, they stuck him behind the wheel of an APC. This was the beginning of his real military duty. True, he never forgot that night battle with the camels, nor about that first bullet, which had missed him by a hair's breadth . . .

◀   ◀   ◀

The mine-detecting group had forged ahead. As usual, the sappers were tardy with their report. The commander of the motorized infantry battalion, a squat, dour major from Armenia, waited until two report periods had elapsed, and then ordered: forward!

Nikolai's APC was at the head of the column. The motor was pulling beautifully, and the ride was sheer pleasure. In the tiny cabin, right in front of Nikolai's eyes, hung a photo of a gypsy-looking girl. She was quite naked, and sprawled with her arms and legs wide apart on a synthetic mattress.

This photo had belonged to Nikolai's predecessor, who had served his term and returned home to Alma-Ata, leaving the gypsy beauty behind. The officers in their group were always trying, without success, to hijack that photo. The result was that the gypsy beauty had, at one time or another, graced the interiors of all the APCs, like a trusty comrade-in-arms, and then finally returned to her original home. When Nikolai's APC hit an English T-6.1 mine, the photo was torn from its place. The mine had been buried too deep to be detonated by the first sapper-filled APC but was ready to explode by the time Nikolai's APC rolled over it. Nikolai was catapulted halfway out of the hatch. His elbow pressed against its rim, deafened by the explosion, he clambered out onto the armor. The soldiers riding on top had all been flung to the ground, and were beginning to pick themselves up, rubbing painful spots and dusting themselves. There were no serious injuries.

Riding outside, on the armor of the transports, was a matter of life or death in Afghanistan. Should the vehicle strike a mine, the soldiers would be flung clear, just as on this occasion. Whereas those who rode inside—for instance, in the paratroop groups—would buy instant death. There had been all too many such cases. The best scientific brains had spent decades trying to make the armor impenetrable. The best engineers and workmen were engaged in its production. But here, in Afghanistan, it suddenly became useless, and even a downright danger to those whom it was supposed to protect.

Of course, it was so only in motion and when it set off a mine or was subjected to direct grenade attack. But the war in Afghanistan was one in which mines were deployed more than in just about any other conflict.

The sappers looked over the site and came to the conclusion that they had been plain lucky. At the last moment, for some reason known only to himself, the driver had veered a little to one side, away from the head of the mine. Otherwise, said one of the sappers, the full force of the explosion would have been slap in the middle of the base of the vehicle, and it would have been curtains for everyone.

Nikolai didn't know what had made him veer to the side, and nobody asked him. Just like nobody had asked him about that bullet that had just missed him. Or from which he had crawled away, call it what you will.

He remembered that mine for a long time. Not because he had been lucky, though, but because the photo of the gypsy girl, which had become a sort of good-luck charm, disappeared without a trace.

◀   ◀   ◀

On the eve of another incident he received a letter from Zagorsk. It was from a girl he'd been seeing before he was drafted into the army. Not the one who had wanted to drag him into bed—he thought about her with increasing frequency here—but another one, who was not bad either, but serious.

"Dear Nikolai," wrote Nina, "We had another funeral here the other day; Sasha Morozov, you'll remember him, of course. His body was shipped back from Afghanistan. I'm terribly worried about you. I never thought I'd be like this. Sasha's father has gone to Moscow. At the funeral he was shouting that if only the Afghans are fighting in Afghanistan, the way the papers claim, let them explain to him in Moscow why it's our boys who get sent back in coffins. You know, Kolya, there's so much I can't understand, but I keep my mouth shut. I saw your mother a few days ago. She's doing her best to bear up. I promise you that I'll give her as much moral support as I can. Your Nina."

The letter upset Nikolai very much. Certainly he knew Sasha Morozov. So Sasha had been here too, maybe even quite nearby. They had not been close friends, but in that moment it seemed to Nikolai that there was nobody he cared for more.

But grief for his hometown acquaintance was swept away by a loss in his own platoon. Right in front of their eyes a sniper from an Afghan village killed Volodya Korneyev—everybody's favorite, the best joke-teller in the entire "limited contingent" of Soviet forces. The bullet got him right in the temple. All those who'd been laughing at his jokes that very morning were now crying unashamedly.

It was a ghastly sight.

The lieutenant colonel was in a raging fury.

The remains of the village smoldered in the sun.
The barrels of three BMP* guns cooled slowly. . . .

◄   ◄   ◄

The following evening Nikolai was returning from Ba-
gram in his APC, with just the crew on board. They by-
passed the combined antitank and antipersonnel
minefields, and negotiated the most dangerous spot (col-
loquially known as the "green belt") without incident.
Two stray rocket missiles whistled by harmlessly. On one
of the sharp turns, the telescopic antenna that cut
through the air above the APC slashed a branch of an
overhanging tree. A deafening explosion echoed around
the valley, sending stabs of pain through the soldiers' eardrums. Despite its weight of many tons, the APC was
flung forward like an empty tub. Nikolai did not try to
brake, but, on the contrary, increased speed.

Their first thought was that they'd been hit by a
grenade, but some 300 to 500 meters farther on Nikolai
slowed down. He had quickly abandoned the civilian
habit of pulling to the side of the road to stop, thank
God. The likelihood of mines along the road's edge is not
an attractive prospect.

They examined their vehicle. No dents, no holes.

The valley looked deserted, apart from the usual
couple of vultures soaring above. Another sat on the
ground not far off, with a wet, pink beak. They'd interrupted its revolting feast. The remains of a village clung
to the side of a hill, but it was too far away for the attack

*Infantry fighting vehicles.

to have come from there. And anyway, you could tell that our boys had done a pretty thorough job on it.

"It seems as though that explosion was right above us," remarked someone.

"Yes, but it wasn't a rocket."

"I thought the explosion came from overhead, too," said Nikolai. "I don't know what made the APC career like that, but it did. I felt it. It was even lifted off the ground."

The mystery was solved by the radio operator.

"It's my equipment that caused it," he said. "For sure."

The radio antenna was, indeed, responsible.

There had been a mine fixed to the tree branch, and the antenna had hit it, setting it off. The mine had been put there with APC radio antennas in mind: they were long and flexible, striking branches and rocky overhangs on the mountain roads. Like every successful wartime ploy, this new hazard quickly spread throughout the whole region.

"If we'd been going any slower, we'd be dead meat," pronounced the radio operator.

Nikolai remembered quite clearly that, for some reason, he had increased speed going into that turn instead of slowing down. It was that that saved them. As always he had acted instinctively. The APC had caught the edge of the explosion; its full force would have hit the basalt blocks and maybe uprooted the tree: you couldn't see from here.

While his companions relieved themselves right there by the APC, Nikolai recalled the other mine he had "located" not long ago. Then his thoughts returned to this latest one. I bet the next one will be under my pillow, he said to himself.

But up until now, divine intervention seemed to be on his side.

◄   ◄   ◄

A letter from Nina arrived right in the middle of preparations for a very difficult forced march.

"I don't know whether time flies or drags where you are," she wrote, "but here it simply stands still! Every day is like a year. The disco that was opened while you were still here has been closed. I didn't go there myself, but heard about it. I'm working at the television factory now. In the first place, it brings me thirty rubles more. Secondly, it's all modern—electronics, new equipment. In other words, I have some prospects at last. What they say about Afghanistan here doesn't sound too good. I never used to listen to Voice of America or the BBC, but I do now. Some of the things they say are really terrible. Not that I believe them, of course. But even the things in our papers and on our radio have me confused: if everything in Afghanistan is so normal, what are you all doing there? Of course, you will know and understand much more than I do. But it would be so much better if you were here! I phoned your mother. She says that her life is pure suffering while you're in Afghanistan. That's true. I daresay it's the same for your father. And I'm not made of steel, either. Nina."

He knew. He understood.

Yes, he knew. And, naturally, he saw a great deal more than all his contemporaries in Zagorsk taken together. He saw the dead, ruined villages along the roads—oh, so many of them! He encountered Afghan peasants—

probably the most oppressed and poor creatures on earth, with their inevitable wooden plows and primitive hoes. He had peered into damp, mud-brick huts filled with dirty, ragged children, who darted around with the feral speed of rodents.

Yes, he saw. But seeing and understanding are two different things. All that he had seen did not come together into an integral, meaningful picture in his mind. It was all fragments of an alien and, in many ways, frightening existence. No more than that. But the war, strangely enough, was not alien. Because he was surrounded by his own people, and they were all equally involved. They were all united by a simple and clear aim: to do battle. To destroy those they were told to destroy. And to repel those who attacked them.

The words revolution and internationalism did not, as concepts, arouse any special emotions in Nikolai's breast—neither positive nor negative ones. Admittedly, when he heard them on the parade ground, standing in line with flags flying and music playing, he did experience something akin to emotional uplift. That was so. And felt himself to be a defender of something elevated and necessary. But that was only on the parade ground. Not when he was just by himself.

Ideas and causes were heady wine to others. He was merely a conscientious, reliable, ordinary soldier.

◀　　◀　　◀

The hill was just like any other hill. They decided to stop here. But three APCs, including Nikolai's, were ordered to proceed farther, so they moved off.

A staff interpreter sat next to Nikolai; they had only met on the way. The interpreter was a young fellow called Sikander, a Tadzhik from Dushanbe. He was surly and uncommunicative.

Nikolai was not in the habit of prying into other people's business, but he asked whether anything was wrong.

"It's my birthday today," answered the other briefly, and relapsed into morose silence.

"Well, you can celebrate later," remarked Nikolai bracingly.

They saw the foxholes simultaneously, but assumed them to be "ours." Even though Intelligence didn't make any mention of their own people being in the vicinity. Still, it couldn't be spooks—they don't dig in. They had their "kirizes," which took a heavy toll on men and technology. Retaliation had little effect; it was just carried out to make reports to headquarters look good. Artillery fire was useless.

Attacks on Soviet armored groups were usually carried out without any prior warning. The spooks would emerge out of camouflaged manholes and open fire. Then they would disappear into the depths of their "kirizes," a network of underground tunnels dug for irrigation purposes, but now serving as perfect bolt holes. Some of the tunnels were large enough to allow movement of vehicles as well as people. They stretched under fields, alongside roads, and underneath villages. Kirizes under villages drove the Soviet soldiers mad. One minute you'd have concentrated fire coming from a village, but when you entered it, there wouldn't be a soul to be seen: everyone would have gone to ground in the kirizes, and the village would be deserted.

And you wouldn't find anyone, try as you might.

But these were ordinary foxholes. Strange. Nikolai stretched out a hand to report his doubts, but in that moment all doubts were resolved: some 50 meters before the first line of foxholes they saw a spook. He was dirty and bedraggled, like a sapper's dog. He clambered out of a hole and opened up with a grenade launcher. The first shot ricocheted off Nikolai's APC and exploded a little way ahead. The next one hit the turret dead-on.

God, they were disarmed!

"Turn, turn!" yelled Sikander. "Turn left!"

But Nikolai didn't need any prompting, he was already doing just that. He saw that one of his boys had been killed; smoke billowed around the turret.

"Hurry!" shouted the interpreter. "It's an ambush! There's lots of them!"

And there did seem to be a lot of spooks, all toting grenade launchers and submachine guns.

Another missile went under the front wheels and exploded below the first axle. A searing flame burst through from under Nikolai's seat. He felt his entire back to be on fire. Although swearing was an integral part of daily life in Afghanistan, even in the presence of officers, Nikolai had never really mastered the art. So now he sat and howled with pain.

The vehicle stopped, and wouldn't respond to the steering column. It was imperative to get out somehow. Sikander was already out of the cabin. But Nikolai was swathed in flames. He beat at them, then seized the wheel, frantically pressing all the pedals in an effort to turn the APC. His undershirt was melting against his skin; the pain was becoming unbearable. Paint and wiring burned all around him, but he just kept on trying. He simply couldn't imagine losing the APC. What would happen then?

"Two seconds, one, half a second," a voice intoned relentlessly in his head, drowning out the explosions outside.

No seconds left!

He rolled out onto the body of the vehicle—awful, awful—everything burning all around, no sign of any of the others, just the chatter of automatic fire. He fell to the ground just as two missiles turned the APC into a useless heap of metal. But the APC served him one last good turn by offering him concealment behind its twisted armor. The most important thing was that he'd got out of it in time. Just like he had evaded the bullet that had brought death's greeting so close, just like the times with those treacherous mines.

Now he had to get himself over to the second APC. The others had rallied and were firing desperately from it. He caught a bullet in the side on his way across, but luckily it was just a flesh wound. The childish misapprehension that a bullet is only small, it can't get all of me, seemed right. The bullet had not hit "all of him." He ran.

Nobody who describes a battle in which he did not take part, did not burn, get wounded, shoot, see friends die before his eyes, did not dodge among burning, twisted metal, can convey the most important thing of all: the feelings of those who did take part.

Amazingly enough, there are very few soldiers who did burn in battle, suffered, lost their friends before their eyes, who can later give an accurate account of their feelings at that time. Even though such moments are the most important ones of their lives. It is not likely that they will ever be repeated; most probably they won't. Afterwards, life is lost, or becomes dull, like working on a conveyer belt in a factory.

But the words won't come!

Memory retains only movements: jumped, ran, crouched, shot, saw, fell.

Nikolai ran.

Four of the paratroopers on his pal Sergei Struve's APC were already dead. They sat immobile amid the general chaos, leaning against the APC's turret, as though taking a rest—horrible, horrible. Sergei was trying to maneuver his vehicle just as Nikolai had, before his APC had been reduced to a pile of junk. Scrambling up onto the armor with those who were still alive, including some crew members from the third APC, Nikolai opened fire on the foxholes.

But then a grenade hit their fuel tank. My God, what started then! The APC burst into flame like a powder magazine. Nikolai's friend Sergei managed to clamber out, but—what a ghastly day, what a black day it was!— a direct bullet and flames, burning fuel, and that was it, the end. The sharpshooter and the radio operator were killed outright. A black day indeed.

There were more hits, more deaths. And now this APC—the second one in the past ten minutes of Nikolai's life—shook and roared from striking missiles and flame. For the second time in this brief, fierce battle he heard some unseen chronometer in his head counting: "one second, half a second, none!"

Rolling off the burning armor onto the burning earth, he sprinted for a nearby cemetery. Men from the third APC, which was also engulfed in flame, ran, weaved, and fell beside him, shooting as best they could. A long, mud-brick wall ran alongside the cemetery. There was a break in the wall.

It didn't take the spooks a minute to figure out what was what, and they surged forward in pursuit. But they weren't fast enough, and encountered a barrage. The short barrels of submachine guns spewed out thousands of bullets. The spooks were demented, throwing themselves into the direct line of fire, anything to get through. Their guns chattered constantly, too. Bullets whistled over heads and graves. The dead were protected by Death, the living by one mud-brick wall.

The battle intensified. Knowing the weakness of their position and the overwhelming numbers of the spooks, the *shuravi* began to retreat. The junior officer from the third APC issued brief, hoarse orders:

"Bellies to the ground! First three—go on, crawl! Along the wall, along the wall!" he shouted.

As each group crawled off, the others gave them covering fire. Nikolai, it seemed, would be the fifth to go. His clothes were in tatters. At headquarters they believed that a soldiers should get at least six months' wear out of his uniform.

He huddled up to the wall.

"Bastards!" yelled the junior officer, shooting at will. "Filthy bastards! Sons of bitches!"

Support came from the hill, where the main group had halted. An APC made it to the cemetery, and took them on board.

"That was one for the books!" reiterated the junior officer, whose voice was all but gone from shouting. "That was some ambush!" He shook his head dazedly on a bull-like, blood-covered neck.

On the way back up the hill, Nikolai was not conscious of any pain. He forgot all about his burned back and the bullet wound. There can be moments of rejoicing even in battle: the APC—their savior—was an object of joy. So is a rut, which offers a bit of shelter. So is a cemetery wall. As is the cemetery itself, with multicolored rags flapping on spikes. There is only happiness, only good in wartime. That which is bad, is still. And omnipresent.

. . . There was a whole platoon on the hill, firing at the spooks with heavy machine guns and two howitzers.

The wounded lay and sat against the dusty protectors of heavy Ural trucks. When Nikolai was eased back against this thick, corrugated rubber, he almost fainted. Pain seared his back. The crash of firearms made it impossible to distinguish the voices of his friends—how many of them were still alive?—and all he could make out was the voice of the senior lieutenant, who sat there with a smashed-up face and kept repeating, like a broken record: "Sorry, lads. I was the one who made you go there. It's all my fault."

With the appearance of Mi-24 helicopters, the situation was reversed: now it was the spooks' turn to find themselves in hell. The choppers swooped over the line of foxholes—so you want to fight European style, do you?—spitting out pinkish-blue streaks of fire and missiles. Mud, sand, and rocks fountained up, showered down on the trenches, and obscured the sky.

The earth groaned with explosions and gave birth to dead men.

Revenge brought little satisfaction to those who lay beside the Urals. Among those whose bodies had been stacked near the first cross-country vehicle Nikolai saw his erstwhile traveling companion, Sikander the interpreter. He didn't seem to be breathing. Bought it. He lay on his back, face to the sky, ramrod straight as if at attention. Just the way living soldiers draw themselves up when receiving decorations on parade.

Dead on his birthday. As though he'd never been born.

The wounded were waiting for the arrival of medical choppers. For them, the battle was over. Only for a spell for some; for others—forever.

◀ ◀ ◀

The heavily wounded were carried to the helicopters on stretchers, while those with lighter injuries were dragged across by the arms. Nikolai reeled over unaided. They treated his back, bandaged it tightly, but it seemed to burn as though he were still inside his flaming APC. The bullet wound in his side became increasingly painful, too. There was a roaring in his ears, interspersed by periods of dead silence.

Staggering across the sand, he tried to decide which of the two choppers was the better choice—the first or the second.

The Mi-8 pilots had kept their motors running and peered out of their cockpits at the unfortunates being loaded into their machines.

Nikolai made it to the first chopper. He leaned dizzily against its shuddering balloonlike side, waiting for the heavily wounded to be loaded. Some could not bend their legs, others could not move any of their extremities. These were surrounded by several paramedics, who bickered among themselves:

"Put your end down, you damn fool! Quit dithering around!" Everyone swore profusely. Transportation of the wounded never lacks gratuitous advice.

The moment came when Nikolai could set foot on the metal ladder, but he hung back.

Finally, somebody yelled at him:

"Get into the second chopper, there's no more room in here!"

He snarled back, but moved off toward the other helicopter.

The second chopper was exactly the same as the first, but for some reason he was drawn to the first one.

The last load of wounded was being jammed into the second chopper. Nikolai squeezed in between the door and a guy whose leg had been twisted into weird, unnatural angles. The chopper's blades began to rotate, and everything vibrated, down to the smallest rivet. At times, the roar of the motor seemed to disappear, but it was probably just in Nikolai's head. Then it would grow louder, like an approaching train. Nikolai's mouth was as dry as a soldier's plate after eating outside in a hot wind.

Down below there were quite a few wounded still beside the Ural trucks. But not all that many. Or maybe his eyes were playing tricks against the horizon and the sky. Here, inside this noisy, cramped death-can, there was just them—the halt and the lame, without any sky or any horizon.

Just them—halt, lame, blood-soaked, and deafened.

He didn't even try to move. There wasn't a spare centimeter anywhere. They became a single unit. Each forgot about the life he had left behind, be it in Moscow or Kiev, Tallinn or Tashkent, Odessa or Kishinev, Minsk or Leningrad, or any out of a multitude of towns and villages, remote farmsteads and hamlets.

The whole of the Soviet Union in one small helicopter!

Nobody moaned. Nobody asked for help. But, instinctively, they all sought the support of contact, and even those who were unconscious pressed closer to their fellows.

He stared at bandages, through which blood was already starting to seep, but when the blood patches began to dance crazily before his eyes, he closed them.

The helicopter swooped up into the sky. And then something inexplicable occurred.

Suddenly, the chopper shuddered, as though it had collided with something, pitched over to one side, and seemed to halt in midair. Then, describing an imperfect parabola, it seemed to head back for the ground. But it wasn't flying back—it was falling, falling like a stone. A rocket had pierced its stabilizer, wrecked the metal, and set the fuselage on fire.

The pilots made desperate efforts to pull out, but it was useless. The chopper, with its full load of wounded, roared toward the ground. Nikolai realized what was happening for no more than a split second. But it was in that second that the door, its locks torn loose by the rocket's impact, flew open. Nikolai gave the heavy, awkward parachute on his chest a heave and rolled out of the door, pulling at the rip-cord. A few moments later, fragments of the burning chopper caught up with the canopy of his parachute.

"Dear Anna Ignatyevna and Nikolai Nikolayevich! I am writing to you as the commanding officer of the military unit in which your son was doing his military service. He was wounded in battle, but nevertheless fought on courageously. When reinforcements arrived, the wounded were evacuated to hospital. It was at this time that an unforeseen event took place: the helicopter in which your son was being carried was shot down after takeoff. The controls failed, and it fell to earth. The only survivor was your son Nikolai. He was picked up by paratroopers. At present, he is in Kabul hospital. We visited him recently. His injuries—to the head, arms, and legs after the helicopter was shot down, and the back injuries he got in battle—are all healing well, although at first his condition was very serious.

"With respect,

"Major Lunev, commander of the 3rd platoon.

"Lieutenant Stroyev, deputy political commander. 14 April 1986."

◄　　◄　　◄

He was under medical treatment for six months, changing hospitals and beds in Kabul, Tashkent, Moscow, and the Crimea.

His photo was published in *Pravda* and then seven other papers.

Finally, the efforts of doctors and his own stubborn

hold on life put him back on his feet. Then they let him go back to Zagorsk, to his relatives, his friends, his former life, with which he had forgotten how to cope in Afghanistan.

Thanks to fate and the newspapers, he was acknowledged to be the luckiest soldier in Afghanistan.

His old school held a grandiose reception in his honor. The master of ceremonies was the regional party secretary—the father of the lad who had once planned to escape to the West via Afghanistan. As Nikolai learned, that young man never did go into the army. He became a student at the Institute of International Relations in Moscow. "Why go to the trouble of escaping?" he laughed. "I'll go there with a diploma. Legally."

The party secretary recounted all of Nikolai's adventures as they had been reported in the press. He even remembered to mention that first bullet that Nikolai had so narrowly escaped. And the mines, which had exploded so close. He made mention of the burning APC from which he had moved away just in time, and, finally, the chopper from which he was the sole survivor. After a few words about internationalism, the party secretary concluded:

"It is great good fortune to have passed through all that, and remained alive."

"It would be even greater fortune not to have had to go through it," Nikolai wanted to retort, but held his tongue. When it came his turn to say something, he was brief:

"I serve the Soviet Union," just the way it was said on special occasions on the parade ground in Afghanistan.

When he became agitated, the left side of his body wouldn't move—the arm and leg wouldn't obey commands from the brain. Nina helped him climb down from the stage afterwards. Lots of people thrust newspapers with his splendid photos at him, asking for his autograph. When it was all over, the luckiest soldier of the Limited Contingent of Soviet Forces limped home.

Life in Zagorsk went on as usual.

And so, the most important experience Nikolai drew from his Afghanistan epic was the experience of his phenomenal luck.

Without doubt.

But what was he to do with this experience of luck in his own unlucky country?

Alas, nobody had an answer to that question for semiparalyzed Nikolai Ivanov, former soldier in the Limited Contingent of Soviet Forces in Afghanistan.

The Journalist's Story

---◄●►---

And moreover I saw under the sun the place of
judgment, that wickedness was there; and the place of
righteousness, that iniquity was there.

ECCLESIASTES 3:16

I SAW THEM in the foothills. In the next instant, when they appeared overhead, I clapped my hands over my ears, and opened my mouth as wide as I could. This is an easy way to protect one's eardrums from excessive noise. However, this method was not known to everyone here.

The seven-year-old daughter of a family of Soviet specialists who lived in a Kabul suburb didn't know it. A Mig roared overhead when she was in the driveway in front of the house. Blood spurted from her nose and ears, and the flow could be staunched only by a doctor.

Some of the faithful inhabiting Kabul were not possessed of such knowledge, either. The effect, therefore, was increased tenfold.

In the first instance, it had a psychological impact.

If crowds began to gather, Migs would appear overhead very quickly. Not a single one of them opened fire or mounted any kind of military assault. No, the pilots' orders were to overfly the city at the minimum possible altitude. One pass, and you could bet your boots that that crowd would be totally demoralized. If the planes made two or three passes, then people turned into panicked beasts.

Yes, it was an extremely effective ploy. However, it had to be dropped after the first couple of years, when the insurgents acquired rockets and ground-to-air missiles.

Unlike politicians, journalists look first and analyze later. But there are countries and towns in which a journalist only sees. He wouldn't mind mulling over what his eyes had witnessed, but those sights are more powerful than any amount of cogitation.

Afghanistan is such a country.

Kabul is such a town.

Here, a politician is king of a multitude of variations, a journalist is the slave of what he has seen.

A boy who sold Kent and Marlboro cigarettes off a tray in front of my hotel haunted my dreams at night. He was shod in odd shoes: on his right foot—an enormous, worn-out man's shoe; on his left—an equally old high-heeled woman's pump. His torn, ancient jacket was as thin as cigarette paper.

One day I happened to be at the Afghantextile works during lunch break. Workers straggled across the yard in twos and threes toward a building on the edge of the factory site. There, each one would get his portion through a hatch: a bowl of thin soup and a small piece of flat bread.

That was their whole meal.

Once a day . . .

There are always people who aim to speed up the course of history. Their motto is as simple as their desire: now, and not later. They do not understand that a country that has existed in extreme poverty for centuries cannot become prosperous overnight. That Islam, in a Muslim country, is not just a faith, but a way of life. One must act immediately, they urge. Delay is the enemy of change.

This is the main pitfall of all good intentions.

I saw for myself how much "men of action" in Afghanistan—Soviets and Afghans alike—were no different from those who had acted in other places in other historic moments. The results of their actions differed little, save perhaps in numbers of victims and the length of subsequent social agonies. But what of that? For such people, the lessons of history are but an empty sound. The influence of those lessons is not reflected in the current moment.

The starting signal has been given. That's what's important.

The claim that man is alive until he dies was disproved by that Kremlin master of longevity, Suslov. He was dead, yet continued to live. The unliving intellect of the dogmatist continued to spawn formulas and demands. Once, after listening impatiently to a diffident objection to Soviet military involvement in Afghanistan and its consequences, he angrily asked the waverer: "Do you imagine that global revolutions can be accomplished in white gloves?

"We must provide a sound ideological framework for this politico-military action. Nothing else," decreed the *éminence grise*.

"Provision" was the task of a large group of people. Both in Kabul and in Moscow. The group included journalists and their bosses. In other words, those who wrote, and those who controlled what was written. Representatives of other groups could interfere freely—more influential groups, playing a key role in political and military affairs. "Social orders" were relayed to the journalists in an unending stream. The articles they wrote were edited mercilessly. The final touches would be applied in Moscow by Glavlit* and the central military censorship office of the General Headquarters of the Armed Forces of the USSR. Not a single news item, not a single article from Kabul could be broadcast or published without passing through these two obstacles. Therefore the way events in Afghanistan were portrayed by the Soviet media for many years was conditional, not erroneous.

The situation in Kabul was very tense. I wrote a report entitled "These Days in Kabul." I had seen a crowd of people gathered in a square that had not, as yet, been overflown by the Migs. And that's how I referred to them in my article: "a crowd." And I said that the mood of the crowd was agitated.

The Central Committee official who read my piece before relaying it by phone to Moscow changed the word "crowd" to "group." A little while later "group" was qualified as a "small group."

"A crowd suggests strength," he said. "Why depict the strength of the counterrevolution? To offend our Afghan comrades? To show that they're not total masters of the situation? In that case, why are we here?"

Another piece I wrote was about a soldier who had lost both his legs while saving the life of an officer.

I duly took this article to the military censor.

"What's it about?" he asked, not bothering to read. I told him.

"Chuck it into the bottom of the wastepaper basket."

"Why?"

"Didn't you write a piece not so long ago about

*The central censorship body for publications.

52

someone who got wounded?"

"Yes, but this story's about someone else."

"Yes, I assume so. I let you print that other story, didn't I?"

"Yes."

"And that's quite enough. You've written about one, so there's no need to go on."

"But there are lots of wounded!" I exploded. "Thousands of them!"

"And my limit for the number of pieces about them in the central Moscow press is four in the next six months. Four mentions of wounded. And nothing at all about anyone being killed. Got that?"

One had to learn that when talking about the "scope" of this or that, you had to apply the strategy of a reversed pair of binoculars: with any mention of negative events or failures, the binoculars had to "diminish." Anything positive, on the contrary, had to be magnified, and the more the better.

A pathetic little factory, Djangalak, began to operate in Kabul. Its job was to repair cars. I would swear that there is not a single factory in the world, including those that produce the most complex and advanced space technology, that could compete with Djangalak on the number of mentions it received in the Soviet press or that could match the glowing colors in which it was described.

The explanation was simple: Djangalak was the one and only such enterprise in Kabul.

The principle of "reversed binoculars" was practiced, first and foremost, by the Soviet ambassador. Upon occupying the post of regional party secretary, he became omnipotent in his own fief. But he was also answerable for everything—at least, officially. The highest accolade the boss of a region could receive from the Central Committee was simple, yet weighty: "Everything's in order on his patch."

"Order" was achieved everywhere by identical means: any shortcomings were hushed up, any achievements were heralded far and wide. For decades, rosy reports flowed from the regions to the Central Committee and the government. And, it must be said, this was precisely what Moscow wanted.

Nowadays it is no secret how the political system functioned in the Brezhnev era. Everybody knows. But not everybody knows how yesterday's party functionary acted when he found himself occupying an ambassador's post abroad—and there were many such.

An official of that ilk behaved exactly as he had at home.

He is the Soviet ambassador, and his fief is now a whole country. And that is how the Soviet ambassador in Kabul saw his new situation. Therefore, he had to answer for everything. Not a government to its people, but the Soviet ambassador accounting to the Ministry of Foreign Affairs of the USSR and the Central Committee of the Communist Party.

"Everything is in order on my patch," the ambassador hastened to send assurances, and journalists had to keep up the fiction.

Two of Suslov's propaganda rulings proved to be especially resilient. The first was that "Soviet forces went into Afghanistan at the request of the legal government of that country." This axiom outlived its progenitor and the war. The second, that "Soviet soldiers take no part in military action, but merely stabilize the situation," lasted for the first five or six years of the war. After that, through force of circumstances and thousands of irrefutable deaths, it lost all credibility, and had disappeared from circulation by the war's end.

The transition from total silence to miserly glasnost was unforgettable.

One journalist was allowed to write that a Soviet colonel and his Russian interpreter had fought a battle side by side with an Afghan officer of the government forces. However, when the article was finally published, all mention of the colonel had been excised. Mention of the interpreter, on the other hand, remained.

There was nothing to indicate for whom he had translated, and from which language into which.

No journalist could possibly count the number of times his paper printed the words "request of the legal government of Afghanistan to bring Soviet forces into the country."

But I do remember the origin of the claim that there had been fourteen such requests made by the "legal government of Afghanistan."

"Report to your papers," said the Central Committee representative at a briefing in the Kabul embassy's conference room, "that the legal government of Afghanistan applied to the Soviet authorities . . . nine times. No!" he corrected himself immediately. "No. Twelve times. No, scrap that. Better make it fourteen. Got it?"

"By legal government do you mean Amin?" asked *Pravda* correspondent Leonid Mironov.

All he got in reply was a withering look.

After Mironov repeated his question at an editorial meeting in Moscow, it was suggested that he resign from the paper. He did.

Out of all of us, he was the only one.

I felt very sorry for him. The villa *Pravda* had rented for him in Kabul was some 300 meters from the Soviet embassy compound. In order to reach the embassy, one had to walk down a narrow, dangerous street, between a solid row of dusty dwellings. Every time I left his place, he would clamber up onto the flat roof of the villa, lie on his stomach in order to remain unseen, and monitor my way to the embassy with a pistol in his hand.

During the years of the war, the embassy fence was made higher twice.

The person in charge of the journalists, the one who invented figures and saw to it that all ideological instructions from above were strictly observed, was not really a human being. However, the same can be said of the journalists. Everybody was merely a cog in the gigantic state–party machine, and, as in any machine, parts are of different calibre. With the benefit of hindsight I would say that journalists played the part of rivets. If the body of the machine vibrated, then every rivet had to vibrate with it. And not individually, but together.

Personal integrity remained an abstract concept. In reality, it was as worthless as an old doormat on which countless feet had been wiped.

Reporters wrote what they were ordered to.

You knew quite clearly that the National Democratic Party of Afghanistan was a mass of contradictions. That various factions were at each other's throats like mad dogs. Two days ago you visited a candidate to the

Central Committee of the NDPA, and you could recall his words: they brought a hundred people at daybreak . . . tied them up hand and foot . . . laid them out along the bank of a river . . . tied a heavy rock around each one's neck . . . they never did resurface. . . .

That was how one faction dealt with another.

But the orders were to write about the monolithic unity of the Party.

The revolutionary government reached a revolutionary decision: to give the landowners' property to the peasants.

To the peasants, the revolutionary government was as remote and incomprehensible as a government on another planet. The peasant acknowledges only one authority: the mullah. And mullahs have been saying for hundreds of years that the land belongs to the master. If you take so much as a handful of the harvest without permission, then Allah's wrath is inescapable. And now this incomprehensible, distant government is saying—take all the land, not just a handful of grain.

The result was that the land lay untilled. Unseeded. Land without hands to tend it. Land running wild.

But the orders were to write about the success of the agrarian reforms.

The revolutionary government decided to introduce coeducation in all the schools.

Fathers killed daughters who stepped into a room with boys. Young wives who found themselves in classrooms with strange young men had their throats cut by enraged husbands.

But the orders were to write about the progressive nature of the government's innovation.

The revolutionary authorities in Kabul decided to hold a Leninist communist "subbotnik."* On a Friday, at that: the Muslims' most important day in the week for prayer. Four hundred forty-six mosques in Kabul awaited the advent of the faithful in vain—the faithful were attending a communist "subbotnik." The result? Pogroms, streets littered with broken glass, hatred of the revolution, the Soviets, the *shuravi*.

Yet all the papers in the Soviet Union reported on the success of the first communist "subbotnik" in Kabul. (Praise be to Allah, it was also the last.)

There was a constant demand for articles about spies and intervention from abroad. Kabul Radio, administered by Soviet Gosteleradio, really went to town: "Dear and deeply respected fellow countrymen," the newsreader would intone, "today, just as yesterday, dozens of CIA agents were arrested in various parts of the city, Pakistani saboteurs and their murderous henchmen."

In reality, the question of espionage was totally different: for a very long time it proved impossible to ferret out even one spy. Great was the rejoicing when an American hippie by the name of Robert Lee was seized. Everyone rejoiced—the state security police, the militia, the Central Committee of the NDPA, and the staff of the Soviet embassy. The journalist corps came to life. . . .

At last! At last a single, concrete instance.

The battle was on for any crumb of information. Those who were particularly trusted by the officials rep-

*A day of voluntary, unpaid labor on a Saturday (hence "subbotnik," from the Russian word for Saturday, "subbota").

resenting the Central Committee and the KGB were in a privileged position, as usual.

The Kabul Hotel hummed like a beehive. Telephone lines to Moscow were overloaded.

"Have you filed yet?"

"Yes."

"What about you?"

"Yes, thank goodness."

"Why?"

"Oh, nothing, you'll see my piece later. What about you?"

"Well, I said that all the facts will be announced very soon."

Every story hinted at momentous revelations to come.

It was solely due to technical problems that I was unable to take part in a noisy spectacle. I was held up at the stage when it was being rehearsed.

Lee turned out to be a primitive bum. Afghan mountain trails were the best place in the world to wander through an empty earthly life. This was a philosophy espoused by hippies in many countries, and they had come to Afghanistan in droves. But in those years Robert Lee had been unable to come. However, he had finally made it now.

There was nothing to do but to release him.

Lee never did quite grasp what had happened. "How about that," he said over and over, shaking his shaggy head. "How about that."

Not a single undertaking—be it political or economic—was carried out by the Afghans themselves. Only with the direct participation of Soviet representatives.

The formation of the party and government apparatus was assisted by Soviet advisers. The same applied to the development of the armed forces (which proved to be the most stable in the end), the state security service, the militia, social organizations, newspapers, and so forth. There was nothing innovative about such participation: merely, one state model (and not the best version, at that) was forced onto another country.

This practice is not a Soviet invention. It has many originators and implementers. But nobody has ever applied it with such deceit and determination as the U.S. and the Soviet Union!

Nobody!

On the direct instructions of the scientific section of the Central Committee of the Communist Party of the Soviet Union, functionaries from the Academy of Sciences of the USSR managed to set up an Academy of Sciences in Afghanistan in the very first year. It was a unique organization, to be sure, existing as it did in a country with ninety-eight percent illiteracy.

The president of the new Academy had an excellent knowledge of Russian, and was a very charming person. He was always happy to meet journalists; he'd drink tea and make no secret of the fact that tea-drinking sessions that went on for hours had no adverse effect on his job.

The Afghan system of professional subordination, the pecking order, was forged over centuries. It was turned unceremoniously upside down. An adviser issuing advice obliged the recipient to fulfill it to the letter. The first secretary of the Central Committee of the NDPA couldn't take a step without permission from the Soviet Central Committee adviser. The republic's minister of defense could not issue a single order without prior approval from the Soviet Ministry of Defense adviser. This applied across the board. Even the Central Committee of the Soviet Komsomol* had its permanent representatives in Kabul, who acted as advisers to the Democratic Organization of Afghan Youth, which they had set up.

It was a huge invasion of Kabul and the provinces.

As a rule of thumb, party advisers were Soviet city and regional party secretaries.

They knew absolutely nothing about the east. Their conception of Afghanistan was hazy, to say the least. That is not to say that there were no real specialists on the east in Kabul. For instance, there was Yuri Gankovsky, a brilliant Soviet specialist on Afghanistan. He had been up and down the country even before the sad events, and had a detailed knowledge of the life-style and customs of just about every tribe. But the standard party advisers dealt with practical matters. They were not interested in consultations. As for those who were charged with devising strategy and tactics—they frankly ignored the opinions of any specialist, including Gankovsky.

One of the Central Committee plenipotentiaries, whose mentality would not have surpassed that of a boxing trainer, practically threatened to commit violence against academic specialists. In his opinion they only undermined party resolution, which was the essential ingredient for getting things done.

Gankovsky spoke of his doubts and confusion:

"They don't know what they're doing. They are provoking a conflict which could go on for centuries."

I made a note of these words, which he said in 1980.

*Communist Youth League.

The trouble with the advisers was not just that they didn't know Afghanistan. They did not know something even more important: how to run things in their own backyard, let alone a foreign country. How to drag their native Chelyabinsk, or Gorky, or Grozny, or Donetsk out of the mire in their own homeland. So what of use could they possibly do here? Organize a "subbotnik"? Suggest that the green Muslim flag be replaced by a red proletarian one? Introduce coeducation?

In daytime, they risked their lives. They did so with all the challenging directness of people untroubled by doubts and uncertainties. At night—and I know this for a fact—many of them would ask in bewilderment, as gunfire and yells split the darkness: "What do they want from me?"

Only the arrogant and obstinate experienced no qualms.

But, for better or for worse, everyone was engaged in his own task in Afghanistan. Only the work of journalists, however, was always visible. Collectively and individually, we did what was demanded of us: that is, we drew an attractive picture of revolutionary Afghanistan, not forgetting to project the image of the Soviet soldier as a peacemaker. Of course, I knew Afghans whose devotion to their people was deep and sincere. I knew those who wanted only the best for their country. I also recall many instances of Russian soldiers' genuine kindness and generosity toward the Afghans, and sacrifices they made in their behalf. But removed from the main, tragic truth, even these instances seemed false.

Nobody believed them.

. . . Vodka was drunk in the correspondents' quarters

and in hotels. By the glassful. We saw and understood everything. To many, the only way out seemed to be a kind of schizophrenia: up to this point, I am a human being. Beyond this point—I am a reporter. As a human being I want no part of the lies, the demagogy, and the perversions I accept as a journalist. We're all different.

It didn't work.

It wouldn't fragment.

It all became even more inextricably bound up. Amen.

A Soldier's Tale

◂•▸

"I only obeyed the order. The lieutenant colonel gave the order to the lieutenant, and the lieutenant to me. I only did as I was ordered."

A Soviet Volga-21 sedan sped toward the Afghan–Pakistani border.

To the left of the road, right by the verge, lay deserted tillage. To the right there was virgin land, and it was on this side that a unit of Soviet troops had set up a checkpoint. Their duty was to check cars and carts, to seize contraband arms.

As a rule, arms would be carried from Pakistan into Afghanistan, not the other way around, so the Volga, which came from the opposite direction, did not attract suspicion. But very few cars had passed that day, and inactivity bred dangerous boredom.

Lieutenant Agaryshev, who was in command, was just as bored as his subordinates. He did, however, have an inclination to philosophize: no matter how time dragged in the Middle Ages, he remarked, they passed by eventually. So today, one hoped, would also draw to an end. But it would be nice if it would do so a bit faster.

To the lieutenant, the Volga seemed a heaven-sent diversion: everyone knows that time flies when you're busy.

Later, what happened was ascribed to acute military vigilance.

"Stop that car," ordered the lieutenant. "Let's take a look at it!"

The soldiers signaled the car to stop.

The driver either didn't see, or didn't understand.

The soldiers signaled again, with the same result.

"They're Afghans in that car," said one soldier. "Looks like the driver's a man, and the passengers are women."

The driver's failure to slow down annoyed the lieutenant.

"Fire a warning burst," he ordered.

Private Rashidov hefted up his submachine gun and fired over the top of the car, which, however, continued to move forward. Possibly, the driver had not heard the shots. Possibly, the trunk was full of weapons. In this country, anything was possible.

"Shoot at the car," ordered the lieutenant suddenly. "Come on, now!"

Two bursts of fire raked the Volga. It stopped, heaved a couple of times, and became immobile. The whistle of air escaping its tires was clearly audible.

"Careful!" warned Lieutenant Agaryshev. "They might shoot back. Weapons ready! Surround the car!"

Moans floated out of the car. The soldiers came up from behind and leapt at the doors. The first two doors wouldn't open; they'd buckled under gunfire and the locks had jammed.

The driver sat there with his head in his hands, breathing heavily. Blood stained his knees and chest. A young woman sat beside him. They told her to get out, but she didn't stir.

They saw that she was dead—the bullets had gone right through her. She hadn't even had time to close her eyes.

Things looked no better in the back.

Another young woman sat there. She had been

wounded in the chest, and a boy who looked to be about ten had been hit in one hand. An old woman and two smaller children appeared to be unharmed, but were too terror-stricken to utter a sound.

The wounded woman clasped her breast and moaned. Blood poured out of the wound. The older boy shook his shattered wrist and stared around wildly.

The soldiers couldn't believe their eyes: they had done this. But two of them, mouthing threats, rudely began to drag the occupants out of the car.

"Leave them!" yelled the lieutenant in a sudden burst of fury. "Stand back! That's an order!"

It was impossible to say what caused this about-face: the results of the attack, or a realization of his responsibility for the order to shoot.

They shuffled over into the deserted field, gathering into a knot.

"What are we going to do?" asked Private Markov.

"Isn't it obvious?" ground out the lieutenant, parrying the question with another question.

He looked more crushed than savage now.

"It's not obvious to me," retorted Markov challengingly. He was one of the two who had started harassing the live occupants of the car.

"Do you think I know?" snapped the lieutenant. "Let the commander decide! I'll report, and he can say what we're supposed to do!"

The radio conversation with the invisible Lieutenant Colonel But was strange: the lieutenant's report was hurried and jumbled, while But seemed to be occupied with something else. When the lieutenant, frustrated by the conversation and at a loss as to how to handle the situation, finally asked whether a chopper would be sent to pick up the Afghans, the lieutenant colonel's reply was quite clear and to the point: I don't need prisoners!

Later, Lieutenant Colonel But was to assert that he had meant the words "I don't need prisoners" quite differently, and that from the lieutenant's report he had thought that there was one slightly injured person in a group of Afghans, upon whom the soldiers had opened fire by mistake.

But Lieutenant Agaryshev heard the phrase about prisoners more clearly than anything in his superior officer's reply. He also heard something else: destroy all traces of the incident, and keep quiet.

So that was that. The lieutenant ceased to be an officer issuing independent orders, but became the arm implementing orders from higher up. This always changes a situation, as any army in the world will confirm.

The lieutenant gained assurance. He looked at his soldiers. Locking eyes with Rashidov, he ordered:

"Private Rashidov! Deal with the wounded. And the others."

Rashidov swallowed hard. "I can't," he muttered miserably.

"Then what can you do?" demanded the lieutenant waspishly.

"He can do girls," sniggered Markov, "but there aren't any to be had!"

Several of the soldiers smiled weakly.

"Right, then," said the lieutenant. "Others aren't so squeamish. Markov!"

"Sir!" Markov stepped forward smartly.

"Markov! Do what has to be done!" The lieutenant nodded toward the car. The wounded woman and boy had clambered out of the car and stood beside its bullet-riddled trunk. The old woman and the two small children were just getting out, assisted by the blood-bespattered driver.

"Sir!" repeated Markov.

"The wounded one, she's . . ." muttered one of the soldiers uneasily.

"She's what?" asked the lieutenant, not understanding.

"She's . . . well . . . look at the belly on her. . . ."

"This is a war zone, not a maternity hospital," snapped the lieutenant.

Markov strode off toward the car.

"As for you"—the lieutenant rounded venomously on the still-unhappy Rashidov—"you can turn your hand to something else. You'll bury them. And then bury that bloody car."

Halfway to the Afghans, Markov stopped for a moment and checked the bolt, magazine, and silencer of his weapon.

When he went into the army his mother had said: "Off you go. Maybe the army will make a decent human being out of you. Heaven knows, all your school did was turn you into a bandit."

"But Ma," Markov had protested, laughing, "I was the best one in the school!"

Satisfied that his weapon was in order, Markov headed for the Afghans, who watched his approach in terror.

Markov knew his own strength. But he did not know

that any such strength is but a tool in the hands of a greater power.

Before going into the army, Markov had excelled as a member of the volunteer citizens' militia, the so-called "druzhinniki." He was known at the level of the regional internal affairs bureau. He'd even received offers to join the regular militia. On one occasion he had helped detain a dangerous criminal. Two other occasions were rather more dubious: he had half-killed two young men he'd detained before turning them over to the law. Both turned out to be ordinary drunks, one of whom was mentally deficient.

Markov got off scot-free on the orders of the local senior militiaman. Half the students at the school were druzhinniki, and the walls were covered with certificates of merit, issued by the militia and the Komsomol. As for detainees—well, everyone bashed them about, and they'd get another dose after delivery to the militia precinct. In those days, it was par for the course.

Markov was a child of the times.

... A few meters away from the Afghans, Markov opened fire without even taking proper aim.

The children's bodies jerked and quivered longer than those of the adults. But finally they, too, lay still.

Markov had carried out his orders.

No big deal.

Goga the Georgian and a morose-looking Estonian called Eric stood beside Rashidov. Goga was doubled over, retching as though he'd eaten a piece of rotten meat. Eric supported him, rolling his eyes upwards so that it looked as though he were either praying, or about to faint.

Markov was strolling back from the car.

Rashidov suddenly tore forward toward him. The lieutenant sensed what was coming and his hand flew to the holster of his revolver.

Rashidov stumbled, but managed not to fall. Markov saw him coming and paused. The distance between them lessened. The lieutenant lifted his revolver and aimed it at the back of Rashidov's head. But if Rashidov veered off course, the shot would hit Markov squarely in the face. Markov had raised his submachine gun and waited. But Rashidov plunged right past Markov without sparing him so much as a glance. Reaching the car, he pumped two shots into the dead body of the girl, turned sharply on his heels, and marched back across the field.

"Defenses burnt out; he'll settle down now," remarked the lieutenant, returning his revolver to its holster.

Rashidov came up to the group and yelled: "Everyone, dig! Come on, we have to dig a pit!"

"Snap to it!" affirmed the lieutenant. Nobody needed any persuading: everyone was glad to occupy himself with an immediate task. Even a task like this. If only not to have to look at each other. As they worked, they became a unit once more. And fellow countrymen. A pit was dug in record time. The bodies were dragged up to it, thrown in, and covered.

The second half of the operation proved much more difficult. It was no light task to bury the Volga; this was a job for a bulldozer. But Rashidov found a way out of the dilemma. He brought up the APC, took aim, and reduced the car to a flattened mass with three shots. Burying it was easy after that.

In all this time, not a single car, cart, or caravan

happened by. The ever-vigilant vultures were the only witnesses.

◀   ◀   ◀

If the world were to be deprived of justice for even one day, it would not survive for more than an hour. But the world is still here. Not least because there are always those who will not stand by meekly, but who will fight against evil. Who will fight for the truth.

Some time went by. Eventually, the Afghan authorities asked the Soviet military for clarification of what had occurred. Finding out on which sector of the road the car and its passengers had vanished was the work of a few minutes.

This was followed by a demand for an explanation. Lieutenant Colonel But obliged: the car was a civilian vehicle, but its occupants were terrorists. They'd been killed in battle.

Not so, retorted the Afghans. The occupants of the car had been peaceful civilians.

The lieutenant colonel offered evidence: a couple of Chinese-made submachine guns and several rounds of ammunition. Our soldiers, he asserted, confiscated this from the Volga. In actual fact, Lieutenant Colonel But had obtained this "evidence" from contraband seized by his men from an ambushed caravan.

Why did you not report the matter? But was asked. It is usual to file reports with higher authorities on such incidents.

"This sort of thing happens every day," retorted But, sticking to the story about terrorists. "I didn't pay any particular attention to it. As for the lieutenant and his men," he added emphatically, "they showed vigilance. They did what they had to do. I commended them."

Where are the terrorists? he was asked next.

"Buried," he replied. "Together with the car."

The Volga was duly found. However, there were no traces of the bodies at the spot where they had been buried. Lieutenant Colonel But was pleased: in the absence of bodies, he felt free to say whatever he wanted. The occupants of that car were terrorists, he insisted, producing the Chinese weapons once again.

We have the bodies, announced the Afghan side. It is noteworthy that the Afghans are past masters at finding the bodies of their dead and interring them in a proper place.

After that, there was no sweeping the incident under the rug. Criminal charges were instituted against those who took part in it, and a hearing followed shortly.

◀ ◀ ◀

The military tribunal of the Turkestan military district sat in open session in Tashkent. Quite a large number of people gathered to hear the whole sordid story.

From the first days of the war in Afghanistan, Tashkent became one of the main transit bases. Its hospitals and clinics were filled to capacity with "internationalists." The lively civilian streets of this peaceful city became accustomed to the heavy stamp of army boots. The war, which was only one and a half hours' flight away, touched the lives of all its citizens. Nobody remained immune. Normally conservative Uzbek girls dared the unthinkable: they turned out clad in denim—skirts and trousers—which were allegedly manufactured by Montana, but in fact were fakes made in dusty Kabul outhouses. Convalescing soldiers sat on hospital balconies, looking down into the streets and strumming a guitar to the words of a popular ditty:

"If a woman wears Montana,

Means her man has gone to 'Ghan . . ."

The courtroom was packed with a murmuring, restless crowd. Opinions about the hearing differed sharply.

"It's just a show," said some.

"Justice at last!" said others.

Lieutenant Colonel But and Lieutenant Agaryshev's men, all of whom had been summoned to the tribunal, did nothing to hide their indignation. They saw themselves as blameless victims of blatant injustice. They also realized full well that the absence of the key figure, Lieutenant Agaryshev himself, placed the members of the tribunal in a very difficult situation. The reason why Agaryshev was not present was inarguable: he lay in a Kabul hospital with a bullet through his head. Not long before the tribunal, Fate meted out her own justice: Agaryshev was heavily wounded when his platoon was ambushed near Surubi. He lay in the hospital unconscious, remembering and feeling nothing. Obviously, he could not possibly be called to give evidence. And never would be able to, said the doctors.

For this reason, there were only two accused in the dock: Lieutenant Colonel But and Private Markov. The others had been called as witnesses.

The proceedings were difficult: But flatly refused to plead guilty. He maintained that Agaryshev had misinterpreted his words and was the one to blame. Moreover, Agaryshev's report had been inaccurate.

But's defense maintained that radio contact between the area where the incident had occurred and the command post where But had been was very poor, and that misunderstandings could have occurred very easily for this reason. A test had been carried out, and results showed that communications were, indeed, a problem. Yet the lieutenant colonel had said that transmission quality had been good and that Agaryshev's report was inaccurate and misleading.

Private Markov also maintained his innocence, citing a paragraph in the Military Code stipulating that a superior officer's order is law to his subordinates. "The lieutenant colonel gave the lieutenant an order," he said, "and the lieutenant passed that order to me. All I did was obey."

Markov's defense reminded the tribunal of the case of Lieutenant Calley, who had ordered a massacre of peaceful villagers during the Vietnam War, and stressed that even in America it was the lieutenant who had stood trial, and not the men under his command.

Someone had ferreted out an interesting piece of information: in the Military Code of the Red Army, back in 1937—probably the most bloody year in Soviet history—there was a paragraph stipulating that a soldier was obliged to carry out any order issued by a superior officer, unless that order was clearly criminal.

Now, however, there was no such stipulation in the Military Code, so the soldier could not be tried. Fierce debates raged on the subject of cruelty. The Afghans were incensed by the cruelty with which Markov had carried out his orders, which were themselves cruel. The whole basis of this war breed mutual cruelty.

It was claimed that it was impossible for the soldiers to determine who was friend or foe among the Afghans. Had they not been fired upon by allegedly peaceful inhabitants of villages that they had come to Afghanistan to protect?

Were they supposed to like that?

Rumors ran rife among the Soviet forces about atrocities committed by the Afghans, about the desecration of corpses, about the torture of Soviet prisoners. The atrocities practiced by Muslim fanatics were well known in every Soviet bunker, tent, and barracks.

"So how do you expect the soldiers to react?" demanded veterans.

One of Agaryshev's men, who had been called as a witness, recounted the following story:

He and another soldier had been standing duty by a water pump. At 6:00 A.M. they were approached by an Afghan they knew by sight. They couldn't understand what he was saying, but he smiled as he moved toward them. The two soldiers indicated as well as they could with gestures that it was forbidden to come any closer. However, he obviously misunderstood, and kept coming. Both soldiers had orders to shoot in such a situation, but they delayed. When he was about five meters away, the Afghan suddenly pulled a knife and flung it at the witness's companion. The knife hit him in the throat, and he fell to the ground, choking on his own blood. "I came to, lying on the ground," concluded the witness. By that time, the assassin had fled.

Another soldier also had a tale to tell.

"We came to collect water flasks," he recalled. "They were at the bottom of the hill, and we stopped up top. I was a driver-mechanic. The guys went down the hill. When they were climbing back to the APC, they were attacked from behind. All ten were killed—knifed. And you wouldn't believe how their bodies were mutilated. I couldn't sleep for many nights afterwards."

Yet another soldier described what happened to paratroopers taken prisoner in February 1980, when he was serving in Afghanistan. "This sort of thing was going on even then," he said. "I saw the bodies of those paratroopers when they were brought to the airport, just as our people were preparing to wrap them up in canvas. Their faces were beyond recognition: they had been cut up so badly that they resembled gnarled stumps, not human heads."

Sappers told a story about some drivers. They had been delivering cement to a construction site, recalled the former servicemen. On that day, the men didn't even have their pistols with them. The spooks found out. They always found out about everything. So they attacked and killed everyone. Then they returned the bodies: first the torsos, and later, separately, all the arms and legs. Moreover, they deliberately mixed all the limbs up together, so it was impossible to match them to the bodies. The faces of the dead were mutilated beyond recognition. Women and children had left their marks on the bodies as well. This was not unusual.

Somebody else recounted instances of mutilated Soviet soldiers being gutted and then returned with bellies full of earth and a note: "Have some of our land!"

Concrete atrocities, which were cited in the courtroom and then repeated in corridors and in the streets, were accompanied by theories as to their cause. A war is a terrible trial for everybody, said some. Alongside courage and mercy, there were inevitably cowardice and evil. And the individual is not always to blame. What Ivanov can take might break Petrov. One would emerge from battle stronger and wiser, another would be fit for nothing more than a psychiatric ward.

In sending soldiers into a foreign country, even for the best of reasons, said others, society had to expect such negative consequences as cruelty, callousness, and hatred.

Others pointed out that the whole of Afghanistan had become a battlefield. Our soldiers had seen and experienced all the horrors of such a war. They knew that the front was everywhere, that it passed through single villages, even through single families. The whole atmosphere, the situation, resulted in perfectly normal, decent Soviet lads becoming xenophobes, killers, and sadists. Such is the price of internationalism—it can't be helped.

Some reasoned that there was an immense difference between those internationalists who had taken part in the Spanish civil war in the thirties, and the soldiers who were sent to Afghanistan in the eighties: the former had had mature, clearly defined convictions, the latter were lined up on a parade ground just before being shipped and informed that they were "internationalists." This, they stressed, was a factor to be borne in mind.

The tribunal was unable to find Lieutenant Colonel But directly responsible for the death of the Afghans. A conversation over a field radio is not a written order. It was possible to interpret But's words several ways, especially as it made things easier for Agaryshev to interpret them the way he did. The first order, to open fire on the Volga, had indeed come from him, not from But. That was an undisputed fact. The blood of the innocent had been shed as a consequence of this direct order.

Murder?

The tribunal levelled other accusations against But: namely, that he had concealed the incident from his superiors, and given false testimony, when he tried to cover up his subordinates' crime by presenting the Chinese weapons as "evidence."

Both these charges carried the penalty of five years' imprisonment, and that is exactly what But was given.

However, But didn't go to prison, he was amnestied on the occasion of the anniversary of the fall of Nazi Germany. Amnesty was due by law.

Private Markov was also sentenced to five years in a stepped-up regime hard labor camp. The amnesty did not extend to him—a killing is a killing, whichever way you look at it. He was taken into custody in the courtroom.

Public opinion in Tashkent was outraged. Former soldier-internationalists were furious. Complaints were also heard against the staff of the Turkestan military district within the walls of the Central Military Procuracy of the USSR. Moscow disputed the verdict. But only the verdict in the lieutenant colonel's case, which was reopened for further investigation. Unfortunately for him, further investigations revealed that Lieutenant Colonel But had personally killed an unarmed Afghan civilian. This had happened in the course of a routine flight over the foothills. The Afghan, who was riding a Japanese motorcycle, was spotted from the air.

But ordered the chopper down. The Afghan and his motorcycle were dragged inside. During the flight the civilian, who had no idea about what was going on, was shot by But. The body was thrown out of the helicopter from a height onto hilly terrain. But maintained that the Afghan had threatened him while they were airborne. Him and seven burly soldiers, all of whom were armed to the teeth.

A new trial resulted in But's being sentenced to six years' imprisonment. This time, without right to amnesty. Furthermore, he was stripped of his military rank.

The conqueror thinks about victory, the loser about himself.

But was sent to a prison in Byelorussia. It was from here that he wrote me a letter which claimed:

"I have been the victim of a miscarriage of justice. I am completely innocent. The men under my command disposed of 850 spooks, with minimum losses to our side. And now I am in a prison cell just because I happened to kill one! Where's the justice to that? I believed him to be the enemy! I have two growing sons. What will they think? I have always taught them to be honest and to love their country, to be real patriots. I taught them parachute jumping and shooting. In other words, I raised them to be able to defend their homeland. Yet that homeland has perpetrated such an injustice against their father. I shall continue to fight for justice, and will win in the end."

◀   ◀   ◀

The procurator-general of the USSR also received a letter:

"We, the undersigned, former soldier-internationalists and currently students at the Leningrad Medical Institute of Sanitary Hygiene, are deeply disturbed by the sentence meted out to our comrade, Private Markov. In reaching its decision, the military tribunal ignored the Military Code, which is a totally unacceptable circumstance and violation of all legal procedural norms. When in combat, we all bore in mind that a commanding officer's order is law to his subordinates. We knew that. Did the military tribunal? We demand a review of Markov's case. His place is here, at the Institute with us, where he always wanted to be, and not in prison. He will be a good doctor. He was a good soldier. We hope that justice will be done."

◄   ◄   ◄

Former soldier-internationalist, member of the Limited Contingent of Soviet Forces in Afghanistan, Alexei Markov went to his place of confinement under escort. His new road went past the institute where his comrades-in-arms were studying, secure in their belief in a soldier's inculpability, past the school, in which he had claimed to be "the best." And finally, past the house in which his mother awaited him anxiously.

Her hopes that the army would make "a decent human being" out of her son proved to be in vain.

Turned to ashes.

The Journalist's Story

... an untimely birth is better than he. For he cometh
in with vanity, and departeth in darkness, and his name
shall be covered with darkness. Moreover he hath not
seen the sun, nor known any thing: this hath more rest
than the other.

ECCLESIASTES 6:3–5

Every morning I would wake up and think: Oh, Lord, not again!

White collars, blue flannel jackets with square patch-pockets, creased wide trousers and slippers. Arms and legs encased in plaster. Bandaged heads and necks.

That bloody receptacle of the war, the central Soviet military hospital, was in a relatively quiet quarter of Kabul. Before you could enter the hospital grounds, you had to stop outside a tall pair of iron gates, emblazoned with red stars. A sentry booth stood to the left of the gates. To the right, on the wall of a corner building, there was an immense, colorful mural. This mural depicted manly soldier-internationalists bathed in the bright beams of Kremlin stars.

Beyond the gates lay the yelling, moaning, bleeding property of military medics.

Few journalists—especially Soviet ones—went out of their way to come here to seek the truth. First, they did not want to exacerbate their nerves. Second, gratuitous truth is always so much harder to take than lies, demand for which had never slackened in seven years of war.

I was not at all keen to go there, either.

But then, nobody asks you.

A week before I was to fly, yet again, from Moscow to Kabul, my assignment was changed. I was to go to the Arctic, to the North Pole, where a great show was to take place in honor of the members of a Soviet–Canadian expedition. For the first time, the Arctic had been conquered on skis.

When fireworks illuminated the polar skies, I, too, was given a flare. Alas, it was of Soviet manufacture, and exploded in my hand. Such occurrences were frequent in the army—many soldiers and officers were injured by defective flares and explosives. Bombs, dropped to earth on maneuvers, would not explode, but flares, whose function was to ignite in the air, would go off right in your hands.

But that's in the army. This was a ceremonial occasion. Moreover, an occasion dedicated to peace and sport.

An expedition doctor treated my wound, and twenty-four hours later I was back in Moscow. In another five days I was in sun-baked Kabul. My wound festered badly.

So—straight to the hospital.

Every morning I would wake up and think: Lord, not again!

Twenty-two days in a row I would be delivered to the hospital, with its eloquent mural, in the tobacco-colored Mercedes belonging to Mikhail Leschinsky, a popular political observer of central Soviet television.

They treated me in the section devoted to infected wounds. The head of this section was a young doctor from Dushanbe, the capital of Tadzhikistan, Abduvali Gafarov. He was a lieutenant colonel in the medical corps. When time allowed, he would treat me personally. He would clean out and trim the wound, not sparing painkilling injections, and would try out various ointments that were sent from Moscow on trial.

◄　　◄　　◄

White collars, blue jackets with patch pockets, and creased wide pants filled all the available space. White plaster on arms and legs flashed all around.

Many of the wounded lay on trolleys. They reminded one of mummies in tight, white bandages. Those who could walk pushed these trolleys in front of them and sought out better spots.

Most of the wounded sat on benches. They sat like spectators in a football stadium, under the spreading branches of leafy trees. They smoked and waited.

A concert was about to begin.

Lieutenant Colonel Abduvali Gafarov sat on my right, nurse Galina Sokol on my left. Every time Abduvali finished treating my hand. Galya would apply the dressings. She was an absolute expert at it. This slim girl from the Ukraine was never still, doing thirty to forty, and occasionally fifty, dressings a day. More than fifteen thousand a year.

Abduvali listened to the songs and tapped his foot in time, while keeping a sharp eye on the men on the trolleys.

"The tired sun bid tender farewell to the sea ..." sang the popular Soviet singer Iosif Kobzon. Ah, yes, this is a famous, sad tango, written before the Second World War.

The windows of surrounding wards were wide open: even those too heavily wounded to be moved wanted to listen.

"That there's no love ..."

An American flag waved in the breeze above some mission or other, near an APC beyond the white hospital wall. Clumps of jasmine bloomed by the entrance to the building. Three years later I would find myself in another hospital—a veterans' hospital in a picturesque spot near Seattle, in the state of Washington. I would see fraternization between forty-year-old veterans of the Vietnam War with twenty-year-old "Afghan" invalids whose buttonholes sported Soviet flags. And even earlier I would attend a congressional reception in Washington in honor of the first official delegation of Soviet war veterans from Afghanistan, and those who hosted them in America—in other words, comrades in arms, veterans of the Vietnam War. But three long years were to pass before shattering changes and the truth about two unholy wars merged into a common understanding.

Right behind me—a turn of the head would show him—lay a totally silent soldier. He lay on a trolley, covered by a light sheet.

"Last night," murmured Abduvali Gafarov, leaning closer to me, "two of his friends died. Yes. They all caught it together, and now the other two are dead. He doesn't know yet."

The young man's head was covered in bandages—even his ears. I fancied that he listened with his eyes. By my shoulder, the burnt, bloody soles of his feet stuck out from under the sheet.

300"Are you cold, son?" Kobzon asked him unexpectedly over the mike. "If you like, take my jacket."

"N-n-n-n-," uttered the bandaged soldier, moving his head from side to side. "N-n-n-n ... !"

"Fetch him a blanket," ordered Gafarov, turning to

an orderly with a pornographic tattoo clearly visible on his exposed chest. "Look lively!"

He ran off, brought a blanket, and tucked it carefully around the wounded soldier. Then, biting his nails meditatively, he returned his attention to the makeshift wooden stage.

Artists from the Soviet Union did not come to Afghanistan very often. In the first years of the war they didn't come at all. The generals felt that it was enough for soldiers to wear the uniform and bear arms. So they armed them. But souls must be armed, too. Or, at least, supported. Instead, soldiers' souls were isolated.

So, the soldiers mustered their own efforts. Afghan musical folklore was born. But no matter how good the amateur, he is no match for a professional. The artist sang, and the soldiers sighed.

"We've been hearing all sorts of rumors," said Gafarov, lowering his voice. "They say that a lot of flak is coming our way back home?"

"True," I answered. "But it's not just flak. There's a great deal of debate, as well."

"About these poor sods?" he said, nodding toward the bandaged soldier behind me.

"No, it's nothing to do with them. It's the whole idea."

"Crap!" exclaimed the orderly who had gone for the blanket, joining in unexpectedly. "It's all a load of crap!" Clearly unconcerned with the proximity of the lieutenant colonel, he pursued his line of thought. "Is anybody going to answer for all this? For all this shit?"

"I doubt it," I said. "Not the way things are ..."

"Take it easy," Gafarov said mildly to his subordinate. "That's not what I was talking about."

"But it's what *I'm* talking about!" retorted the other challengingly. "When I get back to civvy street, I'll strangle at least one of the bastards with my own hands, see if I don't! Right there in his armchair."

"Why armchair?" I ask, startled.

"Because the bosses always sit in armchairs," he retorted. "Sit there on their fat asses. And—"

An outburst of applause as the singer finished his song drowned out his last words.

"Love! Sing about love!" cried the audience.

Kobzon raised a hand in submission: very well.

"Tell me why

They made us part . . ."

The queue into the dressing station at the hospital was a motley one. The "walking wounded" occupied a bench by the door. As a rule these were soldiers with hand, back, shoulder, or head wounds.

The other part of the queue consisted of those who couldn't walk, but lay on stretchers. They were brought here from the ward by patients who were already convalescing. The stretchers were laid on the floor in the corridor, close to the entrance to the station.

The two sections of the queue never quarreled. On the contrary, those who were mobile would frequently squat down beside those on the floor and offer them a lighted cigarette. They would take a deep drag and blink their gratitude. The "stretcher queue" was never too long, because the "bench queue" would not allow it.

"Go on, go on," those with bandaged hands and heads would say. "We'll wait a bit and finish our smokes. We're in no hurry. All's well."

And they would sit back and smoke. Not just tobacco, either—there would be a joint or two to go around.

The dressing station was very cramped. It contained an operating table with two pulleys to support wounded arms and legs, an instrument table, and a medicine cabinet. On each side of the operating table there were basins for discarded dressings and bloodstained wads of cotton wool.

Bandages that had stuck fast would be soaked off, and if that didn't work, anesthetic was available. But at the sight of the syringe, most soldiers would decline hastily:

"No, never mind that. Just rip it off. Only quickly!"

Galina Sokol would rip off the old dressings with a word of approval:

"You're a great gun. Just like my husband!"

Everyone knew that Galina Sokol was not, and had never been, married. For some reason, very few of the nurses who came to Afghanistan with the aim of finding a husband managed to fulfill this ambition.

"Hope is my living compass . . ." sang the artist.

Just behind a window of the nearest ward lay a man whose chief desire was to die.

But they wouldn't let him.

He had lost both legs and an arm, and all that was left of his face was a misshapen lump.

He had stepped onto a mine right outside the entrance to his unit.

But they wouldn't let him die. "You must live," exhorted the doctors, as did a young colonel who had gone gray while still in the rank of lieutenant colonel. "I tell you—you must live!" And every time, before leaving, the colonel would promise: "I'll come again."

There was obviously a bond of some kind between them.

Private Sergei Bunin lay in the same ward. The unit in which he had been serving had stumbled upon a large mujahideen group. This group was in fact carrying out guard duty of a base—and it really had something to guard: an arms store, rocket launchers, Swiss ground-to-air missiles. From here, they fired on planes and helicopters flying between Kabul and Jelalabad. Once they even shot down a civilian plane, which fell and crashed on the rocks below.

There had been searches for this particular base for a long time, but without success. Bunin and his mates came upon it by chance.

The resulting battle was short and vicious. Sergei was the only survivor. Despite wounds to both legs and a shot in the chest, he managed to get away from the enemy. For three days he hid in mountain crevasses, and at night stumbled over sharp rocks. During the day the heat was unbearable; it was easier at night, but he was in constant, excruciating pain. Soon, however, he realized that pain was not an enemy, but an ally. Pain restored consciousness. He dragged himself over endless rocks in search of his own people.

Finally he crawled, leaving behind fissures, rocks, thorny bushes. All that time, he was subconsciously learning one of the most important lessons of human existence: it is not the one who is exhausted who perishes, but the one who gives up the fight for survival.

He did not give up, and he survived. Survived and found his own people. It took him four days until he came upon a Soviet defense post. The information he gave was relayed to regimental headquarters. The enemy stronghold was bombed that same day, wiping it off the face of the earth.

Sergei's strength was at an end. He was delivered unconscious to Kabul hospital. And now it seemed that he was on the mend.

"Lucky," remarked one of Sergei's doctors to me. "He would never have made it on moonlit nights. All the time he was making his way it was very dark."

"Yes," I agreed. "He would have been spotted for sure in moonlight."

"That's not the point," replied the doctor. "Nobody can survive with wounds like that on moonlit nights. Moonlight stops blood from clotting, and it flows out of wounds like water. On dark nights, however, that doesn't happen. As a result, those wounded on the field of battle pull through."

Sergei himself explained it differently:

"I probably survived," he said, "because I knew I had to pass on the location of that damned base. They could have killed any number of our people from there for a long time to come. So I crawled along and kept telling myself: I've got to make it. Find at least one of our soldiers and tell him: that's where the bastards are holed up."

He admitted, "There were times when I simply couldn't crawl another inch. I just didn't have the strength, and I'd think: this is it, this is the end. Once I found myself at the top of a gorge; it must have been at least 300 meters deep. And I thought for a moment: *this* is what you need. . . . But I stopped myself. All because of that bloody base: I couldn't let go until I'd told someone about it."

Sergei Bunin's story was simple, like thousands of others in wartime. But it occurred to me that it was one that explained some very important issues: for instance, that one can live without an aim, a feeling of duty, but one cannot survive. Bunin was not merely motivated by every living creature's desire to exist. All that lives—be it man, or a calf, or a parrot—loves life. Nothing surprising in that. But the essential aim to survive is not indestructible. Indeed, it is not very strong at all; its reserves are easily drained. A simple love of life would not have sufficed in the situation in which Bunin found himself. The one who survives is not the one who just loves life and its flowers. The one who survives is the one who acknowledges his duty in life.

It must be so.

Most of the heavily wounded lay in silence, their eyes shut. When a nurse would come by to wet their lips or wipe away a fleck of blood from the corners of their mouths, they would open their eyes and mumble. But for most of the time they just lay there without a sound.

Some covered their faces with a sheet or a blanket. Nobody knew whether they were asleep, or hiding their pain.

Most likely, they were suffering pain in silence.

Nobody knew what this effort cost them. Nobody knows about the thousands and millions of people who bear pain. And not necessarily in war. Not only on its battlefields and in its hospitals. But in ordinary, everyday life.

Very few struggle, suffer, and die publicly. Most people overcome pain and trials unnoticed. Face-to-face. In a hospital ward, in the cockpit of a burning plane, in the darkness of the night above a chasm. This unseen struggle, this incessant, millionfold conquest of pain and obstacles, this desire to survive and overcome, is what strengthens and preserves humanity from generation to generation. It is that invisible foundation that prolongs life and sheds light on its transient meaning. It is the force that protects man, even during the senseless days and years of war.

That's how it was in the hospital.

The majority bore pain and inhuman suffering in silence.

... Hitler waged an acquisitive war in Europe and Russia. And this war fostered the basest, most criminal instincts and ambitions in his soldiers. As a rule, this concerned not individual, but mass events.

That is easily explained.

The war in Afghanistan, which was waged by Soviet soldiers, brought out marvelous human qualities in many of them—probably in the majority: qualities such as generosity, willpower, humility, sense of duty, and amazing courage.

This is impossible to explain.

Maybe this was the most tragic facet of that war. Or maybe of our entire history.

I generally tried to keep my distance from the psychiatric wing. However, I did go there twice. By some oversight, they had discharged as recovered and sane a young chap from Nizhnekamsk, and sent him home. Once there, he killed his parents with an axe, and only his wounded brother managed to escape. Overtaken and straitjacketed by doctors and militia, the former soldier-internationalist just kept saying, over and over again: "Those were my orders!"

I walked down the corridor with the lieutenant colonel.

"I hate them, I hate them, I hate them!" screeched a frantic voice. "I hate them! I hate them!"

The yells were drowned out by icy laughter that made the hairs on my neck stand on end.

"I hate them! A-a-a-ah! I'm not mad! I'm not mad any longer! I hate them *normally!*"

"Come on," said the lieutenant colonel. "It's better not to listen too closely."

"I hate them! I had hands once! Two hands! Now . . . I . . . don't . . . have . . . any!!! None! I hate them!"

"Do come along," urged the lieutenant colonel nervously. "If the head of the section catches you here there'll be trouble."

"No hands! I'll kill the bastards with my feet! I hate them! I'll kill them all! I'll kill fucking Sokolov* with my feet! And Babrak, too! I hate them! I'll kill them! I'll kill the lot of them! I'm sane! I'll k-i-i-ill them . . . !"

Sudden silence. Either he'd run out of breath, or someone had pressed a pillow over his face to quiet him down.

Three years later I was to see Americans who had lost their minds in Vietnam. In America I was to hear a new term, acknowledged officially by American medicine only twenty years after Vietnam, in 1988—posttraumatic

---

*Former Soviet defense minister, who replaced Ustinov and was decorated as Hero of the Soviet Union for action in Afghanistan.

---

stress syndrome. The main symptoms are: mental insta-
bility that causes even small losses or difficulties to make
the sufferer suicidal; specific kinds of aggressiveness; fear
of being attacked from behind; a feeling of guilt at being
alive; identification with those who fell. Most sufferers
have a sharply negative attitude toward social institutions
and state authorities. Constant depression, nightmares.
A characteristic of the syndrome is that it gets worse over
time.

This syndrome, so destructive to the psyche of many
Vietnam War veterans, was totally unknown to veterans
of the Second World War. It is a direct result of wars
such as the one in Vietnam and, more recently, the one
in Afghanistan. For instance, there is trouble with iden-
tifying the real enemy, being a war waged in the midst
of a civilian population; there is the necessity to fight
when most of your contemporaries and your homeland
are living a normal, peaceful life; there is the feeling of
alienation upon return from a far-off front; and there is
frequently a painful disillusionment with the aims of the
war. . . .

◀   ◀   ◀

From time to time, moaning would start up in one of the
wards. If it didn't stop in fifteen or twenty minutes, it
would rise to hysteria. In most cases, this would happen
with those who had been wounded in their first days of
service in Afghanistan. The soldier would not even have
had time to look around, get his bearings, develop some
kind of idea about the country and the people—and there
he would be, minus an arm or a leg. Or with a shattered

chest. Or some other kind of wound—heaven knows, the possibilities were innumerable.

The moaning would change to a yell. The yell into a choking cough. The cough—into weeping. And then the whole ward would erupt into animal howls.

Yes, such things took place.

That which occurred in the hospital during the day affected one quite differently at night. The nights were hard on everyone—on those who suffered and those who listened. A moan in the dark, fevered ravings, even the quietest weeping—let alone inhuman howls and shrieks—became intolerable at night. Everything took on sinister overtones. The smell of chlorine seemed to be the stench of death. Electricity exposed tragedy, darkness spawned nameless terrors. The smell of death, which was not noticeable by day, seeped out from under the doors of the wards, even convalescent wards. At night, the hospital in Kabul became the most terrible place on earth. The followers of Zarathustra, the first people to have "seen" a picture of Judgment Day and hell and shared their vision, back in the sixth century B.C., had looked long and truly into the future.

But those who planned this slaughter did not even see that which was under their noses. One of the wounded once shared an incredible vision with me. In every ward where the heaviest wounded are lying, he said, right there among them, in the stifling miasma of nearby wounds, a bed is suddenly occupied by a perfectly healthy patient. In the first ward, it is Leonid Ilyich Brezhnev. In the second ward—Mikhail Alexandrovich Suslov. In the third—Alexei Nikolayevich Kosygin. In the fourth—Dmitri Fedorovich Ustinov. In the fifth—Andrei

Andreyevich Gromyko. In the sixth—Yuri Vladimirovich Andropov. All of them, the whole lot who had been instrumental in sending Soviet troops to Afghanistan, lying there, surrounded by screaming, bloodstained cripples. All gathered together. And so that they can't get away, escape in a government aircraft, they're all tied down to their beds with army belts. For twenty-four hours at least. Or, better still, for three days. Until some fresh air could get into the Kremlin.

A grandiose picture, no doubt about it.

And yet I thought: even if all that were to come to pass, not a single thing about the war would change. Not one of these people would undergo a change of heart and say: "God! What are we doing?!"

All of them appeared normal only on the surface. Only if envisaged surrounded by soldiers whose deformities lay squarely at their door. But in fact it was they, these luminaries, who were hopelessly sick. Their illness was incurable. A terrible, human illness called dogmatism.

Spiriting them from the Kremlin into the Kabul hospital would have changed nothing. Everything had to yield to dogma, including suffering and death. Death was considered of no importance.

"I wander, in my loneliness

My heart flows o'er with grief . . ." sang Kobzon.

The concert went on. Only in one section the artist warranted no attention, open the windows as wide as you will.

This was the welding shop, where they were busy turning out zinc coffins. The materials had been shipped from the Soviet Union.

◀   ◀   ◀

Not only did I see that hospital; I used to come back from it to my hotel, and find no peace. I knew: there are people suffering in any hospital. But I do not believe that they suffered anywhere the way they did in that hospital in Kabul. For here, they suffered for NOTHING. There was nothing purifying in the suffering of its inmates. And their suffering was innocent—it was not redemption.

Here, they hated others—the disfigured, the gangrenous, the incontinent, and the bleeding. Yet at the same time, alongside the hate, there was an acute sense of brotherhood. Here, they swore and cursed at any sign of kindness. Yet wept tears at some unexpected soft word or gentle touch. Here, people lost their minds, and gained insight. But having gained insight, they cursed not only their own lot.

There were thousands of them. Thousands who replaced other thousands.

. . . Such were, in reality, the "higher politics" of an omnipotent leadership of dwarfs in the era of developed socialism, the "Brezhnev years."

◀   ◀   ◀

A column of tanks rolled through Kabul, raising clouds of white dust. They were heading north, toward the border, toward home.

This was the first of six tank divisions that Gorbachev had promised to withdraw even before the Geneva Agreements.

Together with reporters from twenty countries who

had come to Kabul to cover this momentous occasion, I followed the column from the Balak Hissar fortress, whose walls remembered Alexander the Great, to the center of Kabul.

The route took the tanks past the long—long as the war—walls of the military hospital.

The hospital where they had saved my hand and shattered my soul.

You could see roofs above the wall—hospital buildings, storehouses, and suchlike. On all the roofs of the buildings that housed wards there were wounded, those who had managed the climb unaided. They watched the column in silence—home, home, home. They didn't move, they didn't wave their stumps of arms and legs around the way they had done at the concert. They stood there in their white-collared blue flannel jackets with patch pockets, in their death-white plaster casts and bandages.

The end of the war was almost two years away.

A Soldier's Tale

—◆—

Everything was different here, not the way it had been back home in the "domestic" army. The most diverse, incompatible people here were welded into unity and love by Death. Danger, losses, and combat were like invisible strings, drawing everyone together. The sound of gunfire united all, not just individuals. People who were not close by nature, but who shared the same fate.

THE WAR WAS IN ITS NINTH YEAR, but not a single one of these planes had ever been shot down. Not one of them ever had to make an emergency landing or became the target of so much as a stray ground-to-air missile. Even those sharks of the air, "Stinger" missiles, preferred to pass them by, veering away from a rendezvous.

Eight years of total immunity.

Only Death enjoys such privilege in wars, being truly beyond reach. And now—these planes. They must have been in it together.

◄　　◄　　◄

The washbasins were set up in the corner of a well-trodden square. A scratched, fly-blown mirror was attached to the trunk of a tall eucalyptus. The mirror reflected the barracks, the fireproof shield over equipment, and the square itself, where daily assemblies were held.

Tangles of wire formed barricades immediately behind the washbasins, and beyond them stretched a mined strip. At the end of the valley huddled a mud-brick village. From time to time, sharpshooters would fire upon the *shuravi* from the village with modern rifles, or old English ones of Boer War vintage. In response, the Soviet soldiers would occasionally let loose a heavy machine-gun volley at the village.

The usual crowd milled around the washbasins in

the morning. Soldiers, stripped to the waist, cleaned their teeth, yelped at contact with freezing-cold water, and laughed or cursed, depending on how the night had passed.

Last night had been peaceful.

Only the artillery had had their work cut out for them, and guns boomed intermittently throughout the night. The spooks had tried to cut the electric power line, and our lads kept driving them back.

But as everyone was used to gunfire, it didn't disturb the others.

"There's news from Kandahar—have you heard?" a soldier with an ugly-looking pink scar across his chest asked Igor Makey.

"No," replied Igor sourly, spitting out a mouthful of toothpaste. "I haven't."

"They've opened a brothel," confided the other. And then, so that everyone would heard, he repeated more loudly: "A brothel!"

"Where? Who's opened one?" cried several voices.

"In Kandahar. It's got a hundred beds."

"Rubbish!" snorted someone.

"The spooks have opened it," continued the soldier with the scar. "Not for us, of course, but for their own. Naturally, they're not letting the rabble in—just the big chiefs. They fly in whores straight from Paris. All right and tight. By plane, via Islamabad. Not bad, eh?"

"Pity Robik can't go there," offered a voice from the right flank. Everyone roared with laughter, while Robik— a huge, square giant of an Armenian—didn't so much as crack a smile.

"It's no laughing matter," added the soldier who had

started the whole conversation. "I was at headquarters recently, and I can tell you that our brass don't like it one bit."

"What?" asked Igor Makey, genuinely puzzled.

"Well—it's a political matter, after all."

"How so?" persisted Makey.

"Oh, you ignorant peasant!" sighed the other condescendingly. "The thing is, we're supposed to be in control of the situation, right? Yet the spooks do whatever they want. They decided to open a brothel—and hey, presto, they've got one!"

"So what's going to happen?" asked Igor, drying himself with a short, hard towel. A couple of other soldiers stared at the soldier with the scar, waiting for his reply. He remained silent for a few moments, and then confided:

"There'll be a raid. It's all planned. But there's likely to be a lot of casualties: that place is guarded like you wouldn't believe."

"Soviet Forces Storm Brothel in Kandahar," said Muscovite Oleg Aristov, imitating a newsreader's drone. "I can just see it in all the headlines across the world!"

The arrival of the battalion commander put an end to any further talk.

"Who's our best woodchopper?" he demanded in passing.

"He is!" answered the men, pointing as one at Igor Makey. "Back in civvy street he kept his whole village supplied with firewood."

"I'll remember that," said the commander.

He was a "new boy." The battalion had bad luck with it commanders. One had been wounded, and very heavily at that. Another one took a swig of planted moon-shine vodka, thinking it to be Stolichnaya, because that's what the label claimed. They took him away writhing in convulsions. For the length of his service in Afghanistan he maintained: "There's no trusting the Afghans. They're savages. All of them. And Russians are fools to offer them friendship."

It was thought that the doctored vodka had been slipped to him in revenge.

The third commander had turned out to be an out-and-out bastard: he ordered the digging of a pit, twice the height of a man, and would have soldiers put into it for the slightest misdemeanor. He thought he'd get away with it—the battalion was out in the middle of nowhere, after all. However, he didn't—the whole 40th Army got to hear about it. Headquarters pulled him in, and nobody knew what happened to him afterwards.

This new fellow was the battalion's fourth commander. He seemed to be rather on the serious side, very correct in his behavior. Admittedly, he had a real bee in his bonnet about training. Every bloody day, up and down the hills. Like it or not.

Igor Makey had been brought to the commander's notice twice, both times in a favorable light. The commander recalled that the sergeant had said that Makey made mistakes occasionally, but never repeated them.

And he could see for himself that Makey was a good soldier, and a pleasant fellow.

There were plenty of smart-asses in the battalion from Moscow, Kiev, Odessa. They were awake to every-thing. But you could hardly call any of them conscientious. As for Makey—he was good soldier material. A village boy, but no fool.

"Tonight . . ."

"We've got enough strong backs to break and chip wood," thought the commander, "but not enough lads like this one. We'll put him into the penetration group. Yes, that's it. We desperately need someone reliable there. They can move out tonight."

◄   ◄   ◄

Igor Makey was born and grew up in a small Byelorussian village called "Red Poppy"—Krasny Mak. The house in which he lived stood at the end of a long village street lined with wooden dwellings. A splendid forest began right behind the house. In Afghanistan, he thought about that forest, frequently and longingly.

Not only the construction of the Makey house was sound: so were the people who lived in it. The family consisted of six people. Mother was a dairymaid, Father was a mechanic. There were three working daughters and an only son, Igor.

He was no sluggard, and worked from childhood. During school holidays he would be out in the fields, driving a heavy tractor or a combine harvester. After finishing school and before going into the army, he worked for a spell on the railway, in a large depot not far from the village. A couple of times he was entrusted with driving a locomotive.

Igor was doing well. People like that are always needed. They tend and improve not only their own backyard, but the whole world. They build cities—stone upon stone; dig roads—meter after meter; mine coal—ton after ton. They raise crops, forge steel, build bridges. Nothing would be accomplished without them. Igor Makey was of that ilk.

And now he was here, in the mountains of Afghanistan. Ageless cliffs, bare, cracked, sunbaked slopes. In the daytime glare the mountains seemed merciless, lifeless, and somehow unreal. Yet what could be more natural, logical, and eternal than stones in this land of stone?

In a word, Igor tolerated the mountains, but did not like them. Byelorussia is a flat land. How marvelous it is to look around and see the horizon, to see sunsets and birds against that horizon, forests, fields of wheat.

The highest hill in Byelorussia is the man-made Hill of Glory. Actually, Igor would inform those who had never heard of the Hill of Glory, it is only two meters lower than the hill at Waterloo. Everyone had at least heard of Waterloo!

He knew everything that any Byelorussian boy knows from infancy. It was a matter of national pride that Byelorussian partisans had fought against sixteen Nazi divisions. Partisans! Not regular troops, but partisans!

Igor, too, was very proud of this.

When he was in the seventh grade, he saw the movie *The Clock Stopped at Midnight*. This film left an enormous impression.

From this film he learned that on 22 September 1944, the butcher of the Byelorussian people, V. Kube, died from a mine planted in a Minsk house by a pretty young girl.

Of course, the heroine was played by a professional actress. But, as Igor found out, the story was a true one, and the heroine was not fictitious.

He caught an intercity train, and went on his first independent trip.

In the republican capital, Minsk, he located Hero of the Soviet Union Yelena Mazanik, who, in her youth, had been instrumental in Kube's death.

When Igor met the now elderly woman, he asked her to tell him stories about the war.

By the time he reached tenth grade—no matter how much they talked about it during lessons in manliness, which were held in all schools—he had lost all interest in the past war. He was an ordinary youngster, leading a normal life. He didn't think about the war before going into the army, either. And even the beginning of his military service didn't differ all that much from civilian life. For instance, his parents once received a simple letter, which they treasured very much:

"When your Igor was just starting his military service, that is, while he was still at home, before being sent to Afghanistan, he was once standing beside a very young officer. This was in the training camp. The officer's wife had come for a short visit. The summer days were fine, the sun shone, occasionally there were brief, warm showers. Still, one can catch a cold even in summer. And it happened that the young officer's wife did just that.

"A day or so later your son met this officer as he was crossing the parade ground, and said simply:

" 'That forest nearby is very good. Just like the one back home.'

" 'It's not bad,' agreed the officer. 'What about it?'

" 'There should be raspberries growing in it.'

" 'Possibly,' replied the officer, preparing to move on.

" 'I know for sure that there are raspberries there,' said Igor, falling into step beside the officer. 'I can check, if you like.'

" 'Go ahead,' agreed the officer, glad to put an end to this unexpected conversation.

"Igor found a suitable bag and went off to the nearby forest.

"He was back half an hour later: eyes shining, jacket covered in pollen, prickles clinging to his trouser legs.

" 'I told you!' he said triumphantly when he found the officer.

" 'So you found some?'

" 'Right at the very edge, and even farther—raspberry canes galore,' reported Igor.

" 'Ate your fill, did you?'

"Igor stared at the officer, stunned. 'Eat? But I didn't go there to eat!'

" 'Well, why did you go, then? Just to look at the raspberries?'

" 'Is your wife here?' parried Igor.

" 'Why, yes,' said the officer, raising his eyebrows.

" 'She caught a cold, didn't she?'

" 'Yes.'

" 'In our village it's thought that a cupful of raspberries is better than two kilos of the best medicines. I picked some for her.' Igor extended a bag filled with dark red, juicy, sweet-smelling berries.

" 'Give these to her with my best wishes for her quick recovery,' he said.

"That was the whole episode," concluded the letter. "As you have probably guessed—I was that officer, Lieutenant Smirnov. Thank you for raising such a good son."

Igor had no fears about going into the army.

Compulsory military service was the law, so he would do his duty. Also, there were plenty of useful things he would be able to learn in the army.

Some two months before call-up he took part in the meetings of the DOSAAF—a voluntary society to assist the army and navy. This was his first long absence from home—ten days.

"Did you enjoy it?" asked his father when Igor returned.

"Yes."

"Was it difficult?"

"No."

"Well, how was it, then?"

"Interesting."

"What was the most interesting?"

"The jumps."

"What jumps? Over a rope?"

"Sort of."

"What do you mean—sort of?"

"Jumps with a parachute. From a plane."

"You? Parachute-jumping? From a plane?"

"Yes. Well, of course, it wasn't only me, there were others, too."

"Village boys?"

"Why not? Why should they do worse than fellows from the city?"

"Well . . . city boys could be more clued up."

"That's as may be, but do they go around in parachutes in the cities? Or live in planes?"

"Of course not."

"So there you are."

"And how many times did you jump?"

"Three times."

"Now that's the DOSAAF for you!"

"Yes, it's a good thing."

"But jumping's dangerous, isn't it?"

"No, it only seems like that. And we were given instruction several days beforehand, how to do everything—how to manage the 'chute, how to land, how to hold our legs, move our bodies. So now I know how to do it. It'll come in useful in the army."

"Son . . . perhaps it might be better not to tell your mother about it just yet. . . ."

"All right," agreed Igor. "But I'm almost in the army already, you know. The call-up papers will come in two weeks' time."

In fact, the papers arrived two days later.

◄   ◄   ◄

For more than eight years these planes landed on civilian and military airfields all over the USSR. No unauthorized persons saw them land, because they invariably stopped on the most distant runways, and usually at night. The traffic controllers who talked them down did not know what cargo they carried. But, as the years went by, they realized, and whenever such a plane prepared to land, they would exchange silent, speaking glances.

Before entering Soviet airspace, the charmed planes usually stuck to ordinary air corridors. However, once across the Soviet border, they would peel off to follow unexpected, frequently illogical routes.

But there was no lack of strategy and logic.

Anyone rash enough to ask for explanations would have had cause to regret his curiosity.

It was far better to show no interest at all. Keep a distance. Just in case, it was better to keep clear of these planes' crews.

◀　　◀　　◀

The army is the most populous place on earth. But until you have got your bearings, until you find some congenial friends, you can be driven to suicide from loneliness. No matter that you are surrounded by a constant stream of humanity—you are alone.

You are alone during drill, even though you are on a parade ground in line. You are alone in the crowded "Lenin room." Alone amidst the lively chatter of the "red nook."

This was particularly hard on those who had lived pretty much as they pleased in civilian life. Those whose interests were deep rather than sweepingly superficial. Those whose interests went beyond jeans and videos. People like this found the army especially difficult.

The other category that had trouble coping were the "psychos": these came in all shapes and sizes, there were plenty of them in all the armed services, and their numbers increased as the years went by.

They were a terrible nuisance, as they would frantically try to become buddies with anyone and everyone, and then scatter away like billiard balls in all directions. They didn't look to be miserable, but they probably were.

For the time being, the backbone of the army consisted of normal, well-balanced young men. Their problems were the same as those faced by the intellectuals, only in a less acute form.

Igor Makey knew well that his real friends were all back in the village. New acquaintances would not replace them, and nobody really measured up, anyway. However, he knew that he would need good, reliable comrades, just like everyone else. He had no intention of remaining aloof from the people with whom fate had brought him into contact.

At first, when he was still serving in the army at home, this attitude seemed to suit only him, being at sharp variance with the attitude that at least one close friend must be found at all costs. But then he found himself in Afghanistan, where everything was different. Different rules, different relationships, different emotions. Everyone became friends here. A whole company would be friends. A battalion, a regiment, a division—all friends.

The whole of the 40th Army was an army of friends.

The most diverse, incompatible people were welded into unity and love by Death. Danger, losses, and combat were like invisible strings, drawing everyone together. Everything here was different, not the way it had been in the army back home.

Friendship in Afghanistan was born with the first shot, with the first nearby explosion, with the whistling hiss of a rocket or missile.

Shots and explosions did not bring *two* people closer together, but everyone. Those who had nothing in common but their fate. And if anyone were to leave the circle for any reason—be it injury, or end of service, or anything else—the loss was sincerely and keenly felt. To some, it would assume the magnitude of a personal drama.

In these new surroundings, Igor Makey's attitude could not have been better.

◀　　◀　　◀

From time to time, discussions of a cultural nature arose around the washbasins.

The initiators were usually two Muscovites—Oleg Aristov and Victor Rost.

"Pink Floyd and Kiss are making a comeback," they'd announce, splashing themselves liberally with water. "Who could possibly compete with them in the Soviet Union? There's nobody who comes close!"

"What do you mean?" a fan of Time Machine would retort hotly. "We've got plenty of talent!"

"Such as? You don't mean Stas Namin? He's grown fat and spends more time in America than at home. And the Americans have got enough of their own musicians without him!"

Igor would listen to their arguments, but kept quiet because he had nothing to contribute. And he would not have, in any case. He only liked the Pisnyary.*

"The Machine is as good as anyone," someone would assert. "I heard on 'Mayak' recently that they've had an invitation to go to Paris."

"Pugacheva first!"†

"We're talking about groups, not solo singers!"

*A popular singing group.
†Alla Pugacheva, a popular singer in the USSR.

"The Machine has the best lyrics. There's always a meaning to their songs."

"Don't make me laugh! Who cares about the lyrics? Words don't matter in rock, but it really blows your mind. That's how I feel."

"Rock's got words, too. Heavy rock always has lyrics. Social significance."

Time for arguments around the washbasins was always limited. But debates—if there was no drill or combat training—often broke out in the evenings. In fact, they often became so heated that their beginnings in the morning would pale into insignificance.

Arguments were accompanied by such ripe curses that the barracks in Afghanistan at such times did not differ in any way from those of the regular army near Gorky and around Moscow.

In the end, it would all come down to jokes. This was the part Igor would not have missed for anything. He did not fall about laughing, but would sit there for a long time—just as he would have on the bench outside his father's house—sigh happily, smile, and rub his hands with pleasure.

A sapper from Odessa, nicknamed "Kobzon" although he had never sung or finished listening to a whole song in his life, regaled Igor with the oldest and hairiest jokes in the world, secure in the knowledge that they were all new to Igor. And they really were.

On the last night they spent together in the battalion, Kobzon puzzled Igor with a supposedly funny story about a rat.

"A sanitation pipe burst under a house and flooded the basement with feces . . ."

An unspoken question flashed in Igor's eyes.

"Shit," clarified Kobzon quickly. "Anyway, there's this old rat swimming through the shit. Mangy sides, tattered tail, and a baby rat on her back. Right there, through all the shit and piss. Of course, everything around is dark. And suddenly—whoosh!—a bat sweeps past. Right above their heads. 'What's that?' asks the baby rat. 'Ah!' answers the old rat, 'that's—an angel!' "

Igor didn't give even a glimmer of a smile.

"You don't mean to say you've heard that one before?" demanded Kobzon incredulously.

"No."

"You don't think it's funny."

"It's funny."

"Would you believe it?" mourned Kobzon later. "Of all the jokes I told him, I had to keep that blasted one about the rat till last!"

◄   ◄   ◄

Discussions of a completely different kind were conducted on the drill square.

Political Officer Orlov's contributions were particularly frank and respected.

For instance, at his first meeting with the group of newcomers that included Igor Makey, Orlov said:

"You are here on the soil of fraternal Afghanistan. You have been called to serve—so serve properly, without trying to duck out of anything. Learn everything, master everything, understand everything. Your new combat skills, your steadfastness, your new, battle-tested strength, will all serve you in other places, not just here.

The motherland will benefit from them. Life is life. To-day may be quiet, tomorrow may bring battle. Such is the world in which we live. There can be no guarantees: the motherland can give you everything, but she cannot guarantee that there will not come a day when she will call upon you to protect her borders. Such," he repeated in closing, "is the world in which we live."

This speech impressed Igor very much.

On another occasion the political officer remarked: "The army does not only teach a young man to march in formation, build bridges, set up radio contact, drive tanks, clean weapons, and shoot. The army also teaches him to survive. And we must survive here."

"I'll never learn to speak like that," thought Igor wistfully.

◄   ◄   ◄

The uproar had a definite reason: under its fiery um-brella, the spooks hurriedly set up new ammunition and military matériel dumps in countless caves and fissures.

One such cave was located by the local Afghan forces' scouts. After money changed hands, naturally.

The ammunition store was supposed to be a big one, but the question was how to get to it. And then blow it sky-high. Such operations had, however, been carried out before.

They thought that they had taken all factors into account, and prepared accordingly. Alas, things worked out quite differently. The very same Afghan scouts had warned the spooks—receiving payment from them too, of course.

So preparations were made by both sides.

The spooks appeared just before dawn, in the cold, murky light of the small hours.

None of the lads really slept, but dozed intermittently. The shouts of a sentry and the rattle of gunfire brought everyone to their feet, even though nobody realized at once just what was happening. Aristov and Rost's first thought was that the sergeant had picked a lousy time to check everyone's vigilance.

Igor was the one who felt best, because back in the village everybody was up and doing at this hour. But he, too, could not quite grasp what was going on. The spooks had appeared so suddenly. And from where? The sentries posted on the track last night had raised no alarms. Nor did they do so now. Surely the spooks couldn't have come from the direction of the cave, because it was backed by a sheer drop and faced an impassable chasm. Even a monkey couldn't negotiate that. But the spooks were attacking, and there was no time to wonder how and when they had gotten through. If he'd had more time to think about it, Igor would have realized that neither the drop nor the chasm were insurmountable obstacles for the spooks. At home, ropes were often used to assist in various tasks. And the spooks were past masters at using ropes.

There were at least twenty of them, maybe more—in the dim light it was impossible to be sure. They shot at random and screamed abuse. Gunfire intensified.

"Fall back to the trail, lads, back to the trail!" Igor heard a shouted command. Rost fell badly and hit his head on a protruding rock, but his helmet stayed in place.

"Retreat together! Keep together!" the same voice yelled. "Return fire! Return fire!"

Seven *shuravi*, retreating to the trail, opened return fire. The trail was a narrow one, and the soldiers kept bumping into and hampering each other. Moreover, despite the mad shouting of the spooks, none of them could force himself to an equal pitch of fury. They were totally at a loss, and this paralyzed their reactions. The darkness, the cold, and the very unreality of what was happening disoriented them. That's what bloody dawn means, Aristov was to complain later, and the altitude! We never had enough oxygen, we always felt nauseous in those fucking mountains!

He was right.

They were being forced back; two had been wounded; Rost was covered in blood. It was clear that in a few more minutes the spooks would surge forward in attack. And kill everyone. Or, God forbid, take them prisoner.

Igor was the first to understand this.

He had a grenade launcher, but only one grenade. He must have realized that if he fired that grenade at the spooks, he might either miss altogether or take care of only a few of them.

He dropped back behind the others, stopped beside a puny-looking tree, and tested its branches. Finding the strongest one, he used his belt to tie the grenade to it, paying no heed to the bullets whistling around him. He dug into his pocket and pulled out a piece of cord—villagers and soldiers always carry a lot of useful bits and pieces. He looped the cord loosely around the ring. Having made these hasty preparations, he turned to face the oncoming, shadowy forms of the spooks. They came at a run. Echoes of gunfire rebounded from cliff to cliff, mingling with the yells of the spooks; it seemed to Makey that he could hear familiar voices, calling him by the pet name of his early childhood: "Igorye-e-e-ek! Igorye-e-e-ek!"

His comrades, ahead of him on the trail, heard him shout clearly:

"I can see them! I can see them! The spooks!"

A volley of gunfire crashed into his legs, but he didn't fall. And then, when the spooks danced before his face, when he saw their hate-filled eyes and their intention to take him prisoner, he pulled the cord rather than fall into their hands. The fierce detonation of the grenade consumed everything. Fragments of bodies flew in all directions. The last thing he saw, as he fell to the bloodstained ground, were the peaks of the Hindu Kush, surmounted by a lightening sky that stretched forever, even as far as Home.

Igor's six comrades were saved.

That was one of the invisible moments when Death elevates Man above his entire life.

◄　　◄　　◄

The time came, and a "Black Tulip" with a coffin bearing the earthly remains of Igor Makey landed on a peripheral strip of Minsk airport.

By some twisted irony of fate, the coffin was in the care of a lieutenant called Black ("Cherny"). He was a tactless, cynical man.

"It is absolutely forbidden to open the coffin," he told the dead soldier's parents, and made sure that they did not contravene his orders. Only when the coffin had been lowered into the grave and covered did he say: "That's that!" and relax his two-day vigilance.

Not only Igor Makey's family came to the village cemetery at the edge of the forest. The days when the internationalists were buried furtively, like state enemies, were past. Some fifteen villagers came to pay their respects and to support Igor's parents in their grief.

Then there was a meeting of mourning.

A feisty war veteran from the recruitment office was in charge of the proceedings. His civilian suit was decorated with many testimonials to former glory in World War II—medals and orders. Igor Makey, he pronounced, had not died in vain. He had died a hero's death. Those who knew him would always take pride in his memory. This, added the veteran with visible emotion, is something that has always characterized the Soviet people: lay down your life for your comrades! Then, in closing, he said:

"Memory of the material disappears without trace. Memory of a heroic deed—never!"

An engine driver from the nearby rail depot said a few words, too: "Igor could have been a first-rate engine driver. His heart was in that job. We felt it straight away." Then he went on to tell about the dog that Igor had left for them to look after at the depot when he went into the army.

Somebody else mentioned that Igor Makey had once led his class in winning a 4 × 100-meters relay race. The party organizer from the local collective farm, "Fires of Communism," had a contribution to make as well.

"I knew Igor from his childhood," he said. "He loved

farming. He could drive a tractor when he was just in the sixth grade at school. You'll all remember that when he was in the tenth grade he worked a combine harvester to help bring in the harvest. He would have been an excellent farmer. We have so few youngsters left on our collective farm these days. . . ."

Yet another orator hinted that the deceased would have made a good family man someday.

The overall lofty tone was only ruined somewhat by the village idiot, who, taking advantage of a momentary silence, called out perceptively, "But he became a hero instead!"

Igor's parents could barely stand. Helpful hands guided them to the ghastly table of memorial eats. Igor's sisters, having wailed and wept out their grief, tagged along behind. The other mourners followed at a respectful distance to sample the delicacies laid out.

The cemetery emptied.

Igor Makey, former soldier of the Limited Contingent of Soviet Forces in Afghanistan, remained alone with Eternity.

◄　　◄　　◄

Igor Makey had commenced his military service in a unit in the European part of the USSR, between Leningrad and Tallinn.

The soldiers who knew him set up a memorial obelisk when they heard of his death.

One day, the phone on the general's desk rang, and the worried voice of the sentry on duty informed him that "some people" wanted to see him.

"What do you mean, 'some people'?" demanded the general, who liked precision in all things. "Are they military or civilians?"

"Civilians," gulped the sentry.

"What do they want to talk about?"

"They want to enter the territory of the unit."

"Don't they know that that's forbidden?" demanded the general, his voice rising in annoyance.

"They do," replied the sentry unhappily, "but they want to talk to you. They say that you'll allow it . . . They've got flowers, and a bride with them. . . ."

"Let me talk to them!" commanded the general

"Comrade general!" came a firm voice over the wire. "I am a bridegroom, but a former soldier. I've just been married, and I'm here with my bride. We've come a long way."

"Congratulations."

"Thank you. But we'd like to enter the compound. We want to leave flowers at the memorial to Igor Makey. I served with him in Afghanistan. Two of us who are here right now owe our lives to him."

The general was somewhat flustered but gathered himself together quickly.

"Give the phone to the sentry."

"Let them all through," he ordered. "And give them an escort! Take them to Makey's monument, and make sure that the newlyweds are properly congratulated on their marriage!"

Sergei Rusakov—formerly a sapper known to all and sundry as "Kobzon" and who fed Igor Makey ancient jokes—accompanied by Muscovites Oleg Aristov and Victor Rost, both with the dilated pupils and moist eyes of drug addicts, covered Makey's monument with flowers, stared for a while at the unresponsive black stone, and then tugged the bride by her sleeve:

"Come on," they said. "There's no bringing anything back."

The Journalist's Story

There is an evil which I have seen under the sun, as an error which proceedeth from the ruler.

ECCLESIASTES 10:5

I STILL WANT TO UNDERSTAND the people involved in this war. I must find out just how much brighter than I are those who affirm that they already understand this war and those who fight it. How much more perceptive than I, who understands far from everything.

I want to find out the state of mind of those people.

It is vital for me to see and hear out at least one refugee: What does he think? Who is he? Where is he going? What does he hope for?

I want to understand the soldier, too: Why does he fight? Because he's been ordered to do so? Because he's been misled? Because he believes that it is necessary to fight?

I would like to see the commander of this army in action: How does he do it? What does he really think of this war?

It doesn't take much to attain these goals: all you need to do is meet up with a refugee, talk with a soldier, find an excuse to spend a few hours in the commander's office.

A REFUGEE BY THE NAME OF MIAJAN: "I DON'T KNOW."

Crowds of Pushtu refugees flood Nangarkhar province. Flights out are possible: there's one at 9:00 A.M.

It is 10:00 A.M. There is no sign of plane or crew.

Any trip, from which you may not return, or return changed, begins identically: first you are afraid that it will fall through. But as time passes, you begin to wonder whether you need to make it at all. You can meet refugees in Kabul, too. Why fly? It's dangerous. You might die. You may be wounded and end up a cripple. So maybe it would be just as well if the whole thing is canceled. This is an honest—if wordy—confession. But everyone feels like that. Yet as soon as the flight is available, you will be on it.

One and a half hours of cleaving through the sky. One and a half hours of Russian Roulette: will they get you? Or won't they? Or will they? One and a half hours in the air—and another country. Afghan subtropics. A meeting in a lush garden surrounding the former palace of sheikh Zakhir, the finest palace in Nangarkhar province.

The garden teems with refugees. Young Pushtus with burning eyes. Gray-haired elders in quilted robes and eyes as pale as washed-out, ancient silk. They are slow and dignified, until talk veers to arms. The refugees sit on the lawns, surrounded by beds of heavy winter roses.

Others are less fortunate: they did not make it into the garden, and are forced to camp out in dirty tents along the roadside.

As they recounted their histories, the refugees would keep glancing at the snow-covered peaks of the White Mountains. The Khyber area was like a seething, bloody caldron. There were any number of theories to explain the ongoing tragedy of the Khyber. The most unintelligible explanations came from its direct victims.

But I wanted to hear the voices of the refugees, not geo-politicians.

Miajan was a Pushtu in his early thirties.

"Where are your children?" I asked.

"With us."

"What about the ones who lost their parents?"

"We took them, too."

"There's an orphanage in Kabul. They could be admitted."

"That's not our way. The tribe assumes responsibility for boys and girls who lose their parents."

"What have your other tribesmen done?"

"Gone into the mountains."

"And what do they do there?"

"Continue the struggle."

"Against whom?"

"Those who are against us."

"Have you any idea about what will happen to you tomorrow?"

"No."

"Who started the war?"

"I don't know."

"Who's fighting it?"

"I don't know. Everyone."

"Where will you live?"

"I don't know."

Pushtus, fleeing from Pakistan into Afghanistan, Pushtus fleeing the other way. Afghans, treading the soil of third countries. Five million people dislodged from their centuries-old dwelling places. Five million broken lives. Five million people who have no clear idea of what it's all about. What has happened to their country. Why such a curse has descended upon their mountains, their valleys, their homes, their heads.

Miajan doesn't know. I talked to five other refugees, asking them the same questions. Their answers were basically the same as Miajan's.

That is all I took back to Kabul.

The landing of civilian and transport planes at Kabul airport is unlike any other. As soon as the plane starts its descent to the runway, combat choppers are scrambled to give escort. The passengers look out and see the surrounding air filled with bright, soundless flares. These protect the plane from ground-to-air rockets. Such rockets home in on bodies emitting heat, such as the engines of your plane. In order to throw the rockets off course, the choppers surround the descending plane with more intense sources of heat. So the plane is surrounded by numerous blossoms of bright light, until it either lands on the runway, or, if it is taking off, reaches an altitude of three thousand meters.

◄　　◄　　◄

Back in the hotel in Kabul I switch on my tape recorder. The results of my conversations with the refugees? "I don't know." . . . "I don't know." . . .

PRIVATE BURKOV OF THE "LIMITED CONTINGENT": "I DON'T KNOW."

It is late evening. A guard post. Fourfold clusters of ack-ack guns. The stars seem close enough to touch. Andrei Burkov, a twenty-year-old private.

"Have you killed anyone yet?" I asked.

"Yes," he said. "Yes."

"One? Two?"

"One," answered Andrei. "No, two."

"Maybe more?"

"No."

"Do you like killing?" I prodded.

"No! Of course not. But when I shoot, I don't think about anything like that. If you stop to think, they'll get you."

"What do you feel, when you shoot at people?"

"When I shoot," said Andrei, "I don't feel as though it's me. I don't really understand where I am at that moment, and why. When I shoot at a spook in daylight, I only see darkness before my eyes."

"Why are you here?"

"Why not?" he countered, honestly surprised. "I was drafted into the army by law. And then I was sent here. You don't ask questions in the army."

"Do you know why there's a war here?"

"Sure. Because of the revolution."

"Who started the war?"

"The Americans," he said, after a moment's hesitation.

"What are you, a Soviet soldier, doing here, though?"

"Me? As a soldier, I'm fulfilling my international duty."

"What does that mean—international duty?"

"What does it mean?" he echoed. "Why, it's . . . it's a duty!"

"But duty to whom?" I persisted. "Do you personally owe duty to somebody?"

"No, I don't."

"And does anyone owe it to you? Does even one Afghan owe you anything?"

"No," he admitted. "I heard about Afghanistan for the first time just before I went into the army. But Afghanistan asked us. It's a fraternal country."

"What did Afghanistan ask us?"

"To do our international duty."

"In other words, to do something about which you have no clear ideas," I commented.

"No, why?" protested Andrei, and then added, after a pause: "What about you? Do you know what international duty means?"

"No," I replied. "I can't say that I do."

"What?" he asked in amazement. "You, too?"

"I don't know what it means," I repeated.

"How about that?" marveled Andrei. "Mind you, I did try to find out: I asked the political officer."

"And what did he say?"

"He told me to stop bothering him," confided the soldier. "He said that people should know things like that from childhood."

"The government of the USSR reached a political decision: to bring our troops into Afghanistan. And here we are. Do you think that was the right decision, or not?"

"We-e-ell, I don't know," replied Andrei. "It's the generals who know."

GENERAL GROMOV: "I'M COMMANDER OF THE
ARMY. YOU SHOULD PUT YOUR QUESTIONS TO SOMEONE
ELSE."

The massive desk behind which forty-four-year-old
Lieutenant General Boris Gromov sat was bathed in
early Kabul sunshine. The general was staring at the
telephone on which he had just been in contact with
Moscow.

I gathered that the commander of Soviet forces in
Afghanistan had been speaking to the USSR's minister
of defense. The topic under discussion had almost certainly been the tragedy near Kandahar.

"You've heard?" asked Gromov as I stepped across
the threshold.

"Yes," I said. "The radios carried it."

The previous evening in Moscow, where the Soviet-
American summit was in progress, Gorbachev had said,
at his joint press conference with Reagan:

"A number of our comrades perished yesterday near
Kandahar, and some are missing."

I decided to make use of this dramatic situation.
We agreed that I would hear about the fate of those
missing from a firsthand source: namely, Gromov himself.

"There's nothing definite yet," he told me. "We're
taking steps."

"How many died?" I asked.

"A lieutenant colonel and a soldier. We don't know
anything about any of the others."

"How many others were there?"

"Another two lieutenant colonels and one more soldier."

"How was it that there were three lieutenant colonels gathered together?"

Gromov lifted a telephone receiver and gave a nod, indicating that I should wait a moment. Establishing contact with aviation, he ordered: "Get the choppers ready. Two waves with paratroopers. Let me know when you're ready."

He got up, a sturdy, neat figure of medium height, dressed in dark green camouflage fatigues.

The situation was that three lieutenant colonels and two soldiers, a sharpshooter and an APC driver, had been assigned to an Afghan division. Near the village of Dhil their unit came under rocket-missile fire. It was a concentrated attack, and Lieutenant Colonel Bobrik was badly wounded. The spooks then switched to mortars and rifles. The unit and village were surrounded by insurgents.

They tried to break out of the encirclement, and Private Smertenyuk was killed almost immediately. So was Lieutenant Colonel Serikov, who was giving the wounded Bobrik what first aid he could.

The deaths of these became known in Kabul very swiftly. When the battle was over, the Afghan government troops reported to their headquarters that the Soviet lieutenant colonel and a soldier had been killed: their bodies were seen close to each other by the APC. Both sprawled on the ground near its wheels.

But where were the others? They had been in the same APC: the wounded Lieutenant Colonel Bobrik, Lieutenant Colonel Kryuchkov, and the driver Private Kravtsov. Where were they? Where had they disappeared?

"That's just what we don't know," admitted Gromov.

"What do the Afghans say?" I asked.

"Just that they saw those two, but not the others. They think that they were probably taken prisoner. But . . ."

"Maybe not prisoner?" I asked.

"Maybe not," agreed Gromov. "Bombing and strafing raids yielded nothing. Tried it twice."

If the *shuravi* had been taken prisoner, they would be hidden nearby. The only way they could be won back would be by force of arms. In such situations, the practice was to start with intense bombing and strafing raids, first striking at probable locations of spook bases, and then hitting villages. Nobody and nothing was spared.

After each raid, the airwaves would be monitored with scrupulous attention, in the hope that the spooks would try to establish contact. They did not always react identically, but more often than not Soviet radio operators would hear that the spooks would return their prisoners in exchange for a halt to the bombing.

But this time, despite the intensity and savagery of the bombing, the radio remained quiet.

"That can mean one of two things," said Gromov. "Either the bargain's too tough—after all, they've got a couple of high-ranking officers—or they're all dead already."

Gromov developed and gained in stature as an army commander in Afghanistan. He is a man with a brilliant army record and a complex personal history.

Two small Gromov brothers grew up as virtual orphans. Their mother—the wife of a young general—died before her husband's eyes. She burned to death in a plane crash that he witnessed.

Gromov represents the new generation of Soviet army commanders. Unlike the "old guard" generals, he was much more democratically minded. He cared genuinely about the men under his command, and was not afraid of contact with them. He also made no secret of his dissatisfaction with the all-pervasiveness of the military bureaucracy. He steered clear of the saunas and other perks that the Soviet *nomenklatura* established for itself in Afghanistan, just the way it had back home. Gromov also possessed great personal courage: I had encountered him many times on Afghan roads with no guard, in the company of just a couple of soldiers in a cross-country vehicle.

A charming general is a rarity in any army. But there were moments when Gromov was more than charming, when he seemed to possess more compassion than any priest. Nonetheless, as a regular army man, he carried out his inhuman mission in Afghanistan with precision and efficiency.

If my impressions of Gromov are correct, then it could be said that he was the most tragic figure in Kabul.

I liked everything about him: how he answered questions and asked them, how he listened to reports and issued orders. How he posed military problems and analyzed their solutions. I liked his courtesy and modesty.

Devil take it, he was worthy of another kind of war. Or a triumphant peace.

At 11:20 Gromov was advised that the choppers and paratroopers were ready.

"Move out," he commanded. "Report constantly."

"It won't be long now," he said to me, meaning that the paratroopers would get to the bottom of things.

Gromov assumed that the missing men were still alive, and it was for this reason that he was sending paratroops into that area.

However, he did not discount the possibility that the Soviet officers and men may have all been killed at the same time. Two had been lying on one side of the APC and were spotted, but the others may have been lying just as dead on the other side. Thus it may have been assumed that they had either been taken prisoner or gone missing.

This was the substance of Gromov's conversation with the Soviet minister of defense, who in turn relayed it to the general secretary of the Central Committee, Gorbachev. And Gorbachev had told the whole world at a press conference.

No mention of casualties, even if they numbered a thousand, had ever been admitted at such a high level. But this was a special situation. The incident took place after the Soviet Union had announced its intention to withdraw from Afghanistan. After the signing of the Geneva Agreements, after the main force of the "limited contingent" drew in its breath, awaiting orders to head for home.

All the paratroopers sent to the Dhil village area were also eagerly awaiting their return home. But they found themselves flying in the opposite direction.

Their assignment was to gauge the situation and win back the wounded if possible. And to bring back the dead. If possible.

They could only rely on themselves. They could not order an Afghan soldier to try to reach the APC and check it out. It would have been useless, anyway. He would reply unblinkingly that he had already been and looked.

The only people who continued to idealize the soldiers and officers of the government forces were hopelessly backward journalists, or those who were blinded by dual patriotism. Those who had to fight alongside them knew full well that for every genuine revolutionary there was an ignorant mass that had no idea at all about the aims or the meaning of the struggle. Any opportunity to desert from the government forces was seized with alacrity. Lately, whole regiments had taken to desertion.

Gromov knew this better than any journalist. He was fully aware of the mass desertions. He knew that there were traitors in the highest ranks of the Afghan Ministry of Defense. He knew that the most reliable-seeming men in the Afghan air force openly discussed their future: we've made up our minds, they said. As soon as the *shuravi* pull out, we pick up our nearest and dearest, load them into our planes, and head for the Soviet Union. And that's where we'll stay. We don't need this revolution. In the end, admittedly, they didn't do this. Someone smart made it clear: military pilots are needed by every government. Not a single regime can survive without them. They're the elite.

Yes, Gromov knew it all. So he relied only on his own forces.

"Contact!"

The paratroopers were in place, Gromov was told, but there was nobody to fight. The dead were there, just as Gromov had guessed: Lieutenant Colonel Serikov and Private Smertenyuk on one side of the APC, just as the

Afghans had said, and the other three—Lieutenant Colonels Bobrik and Kryuchkov and Private Kravtsov—on the other.

... The Afghan troops feared to go the hundred meters necessary to check out the APC. It is hard to blame them.

Such was the nature of that war.

One cannot blame the Afghan officers who had told their headquarters that they assumed that the Soviet officers and soldier had been taken prisoner. They were, after all, yesterday's enlisted men.

... The Afghan headquarters advises the Soviet command, which deploys bombers in order to secure the release of its men. Military airplanes kill any number of innocent villagers and reduce the village to rubble.

Such are the laws of war.

... The head of state in Moscow tells the world about the missing men and talks of the inevitability of retaliation.

Such is the way of the world.

... The missing men lay on their backs, faces turned up to the sky. A sharp wooden spike had been driven through each mouth, keeping the head immobile.

The paratroopers had carried out the first part of their operation. Now they had to return safely to base. And bring back their dead.

They flew into Kabul from the east.

At the beginning of the war, the choppers flew as they liked around here, at any altitude they fancied. But then it became dangerous to fly low—the spooks began to fire at them with heavy-calibre Degterev-Shpagin machine guns, and portable SAM-7 antiaircraft missiles, at first supplied by Egypt. The pilots took to higher altitudes. But the insurgents didn't lag too far behind: soon they acquired Stinger and Blowpipe missiles. The SAM-7s became virtually ubiquitous. This arsenal would hit the choppers at high altitudes. So the pilots had to go back to hugging the ground. And hug it they did: the choppers roared around just a few meters above the ground. This meant that they were always vulnerable to small-arms fire—and there were enough such casualties. Many were the times when choppers would return to base riddled with submachine-gun fire. But at least they did come back. An encounter with a Blowpipe reduced them to tiny fragments.

So this was the problem of the moment: to get back to base without losses.

General Gromov controlled the situation throughout.

Most of the time, I watched him in silence. Those days were extremely tense, perhaps the most tense of the entire war. Battles still raged, but, at the same time, withdrawal schedules were being worked out. Columns were designated, routes marked out, times set, security arrangements devised.

There were calls from the Ministry of Defense in Moscow every five minutes: they, of course, thought they knew better than anyone what to do in Afghanistan, and when.

The fuss was enormous, the protection—minimal.

The headquarters staff of the "limited contingent" was furious. Gromov gave no sign of his feelings.

"Approaching base," the general heard.

"Coming in now . . ."

"Landing . . ."

. . . Gromov was back behind his desk, which was now bathed in evening sunlight. He stared at the phone, on which he would report the results of the operation to the Soviet minister of defense. When he received a report that the choppers had landed without any damage or casualties, he picked up the receiver and said: "Get me Moscow. Gromov here."

◄　　◄　　◄

In answer to the journalist's question "How should one assess the decision of the Soviet government to send troops into Afghanistan?" Gromov replied: "I'm commander of the army. This question should be addressed to others."

◄　　◄　　◄

The refugee: "I don't know."

The soldier: "I don't know."

The general: "This question should be addressed to others." I still want to understand how much more perceptive than I are those who assert that they understand this war and the people caught up in it. For I still cannot understand it at all.

A Soldier's Tale

"Pity," said the doctor. "Pity it happened like that. But hope exists even at the edges of graves," he added.

THE BRIGHT, warm sun woke him.

"Good morning, comrade lieutenant," said someone nearby. "It's going to be a great day. Feel that Afghan sun!"

"Good morning," replied Shmelev in ringing tones.

He threw back his light, gray blanket and jumped to his feet.

The soldier fiddling about with the windowpane looked considerably older than the lieutenant: he would have been about twenty-five, whereas Shmelev hadn't turned twenty-one yet.

The soldier gathered up his tools and left.

Immediately afterwards, a captain lumbered into the room. His bunk occupied the left-hand corner, opposite Shmelev's.

"Hi, Doc," said the captain. "I'm ahead today. Looks as though it's been decided that I'm to fly to Jellalabad."

Throwing off his jacket, with its medical insignia, he burst into song:

"Want a bullet in your arse?
Fly to Jellalabad fast!"

The young lieutenant blushed, but the captain went on talking:

"I took a gander at the TV at headquarters: you get really good-quality reception from Moscow, thanks to the satellites. I caught the news."

"Anything interesting?" asked Shmelev.

"Not really. Someone or other arriving at Vnukovo airport, guard of honor, social kisses, that sort of thing."

"Where do you give someone a social kiss?" asked Shmelev, and blushed again at his own words.

"Only on the cheek, and without love," laughed the captain.

Shmelev—a lieutenant in the medical corps—had been in Afghanistan for all of two weeks, which he had spent in a regiment quartered on the outskirts of Kabul, waiting for a posting. The previous day he had been told that his orders were to proceed to Nagman province, but he had to wait for suitable transport. They could hardly tell him to make his own way there.

Before going to Afghanistan, Shmelev had lived in the Ukrainian capital, Kiev. His architect father and pediatrician mother lavished whatever they could on their only child. Luckily, the boy did not grow into an idle egoist, but was an easygoing, rather shy but friendly young man.

He had an excellent collection of books at home, and his pride and joy was a shelf packed with poetry—Pushkin, Pasternak, Akhmatova, Lermontov, Eliot, Whitman. Another prized possession was a huge poster of the Beatles, which he had exchanged for a bicycle.

He took great care of his simple record player and collection of favorite discs, and treasured a beautiful globe, given to him by his father. Globes like that had not been manufactured in the Soviet Union for at least thirty years, ever since party ideologues decided that the world was much smaller than the USSR.

Shmelev was enthusiastic about everything.

"Fabulous!" he would marvel, seeing a Spanish-made bus on the streets of Kiev.

"Out of this world," he would aver after hearing a new hit song by the hugely popular Alla Pugacheva.

"Colossal!" he would pronounce after seeing the latest mediocre offering of the Dovzhenko Film Studios.

The future military medic greeted life with open arms.

There are still people like that around.

Shmelev washed, then strode out of the barracks.

Before its rays could reach Kabul and its environs, the sun had to rise above the greatest rocky "knot" in the world—the meeting place of the Himalayas, Kunlun, Pamirs, and the Hindu Kush. Crossing this barrier, the sun flooded Kabul and all Afghanistan with its light. So it was that morning. Golden light bathed the military base. The barracks, built of pale timber sheets, looked clean and neat. The avenue bisecting the base was so well tended that it looked like something off a picture postcard. The regiment was quartered in a very pleasant area, which was the favorite and safest place for various representatives of the brass who flew in from Moscow to inspect this or that. A general or a colonel, after spending a day or two on the base, would tick off a soldier for an untidily made bed, then note in his report that he had "worked with the enlisted men."

But this had nothing to do with Shmelev, and he didn't even know about it. He strolled down the central avenue, greeting everyone he encountered.

Huge portraits of the members of the politburo of the Communist Party of the Soviet Union graced the avenue at strategic intervals. Shmelev found this a very pleasant sight, as it reminded him of Kiev's main thoroughfare, the Kreschatik.

Just before he flew out of Kiev, Shmelev had a very important discussion, of a prophetic nature of which, admittedly, he was quite unaware.

The girl's name was Yulia. He was enraptured by her, too.

"You could follow in the footsteps of Vishnevsky," she had said, referring to the chief surgeon of the Soviet Army, a member of an illustrious dynasty of Russian doctors.

"I should become eminent in my own right," expostulated Shmelev.

"We could . . ."

"That's already decided," said Shmelev firmly.

"Nothing's going to work out for us," remarked Yulia unexpectedly.

"Whyever not?" demanded Shmelev, flabbergasted.

"Presentiment," she replied seriously.

Shmelev hadn't said a word to her about Afghanistan. So far only his parents knew that he was flying out to Kabul.

"Presentiments are for gray-haired oldies," he answered bracingly. "Nothing will upset our plans. At worst, they'll only be delayed for a bit."

Shmelev didn't know that even eighteen-year-old girls, in most cases, subconsciously know the future fate of the boys in their circle. Their intuition tells them that this one will succeed, and that one will be a failure. That this one is a safe prospect, and that one will bring nothing but grief. And they have an even keener sense of impending tragedy.

The war in Afghanistan aroused enthusiasm, not fear, in Shmelev.

"I'm certain that we'll be together," he stated.

"You're a military man," said Yulia, "a lieutenant."

"I'm a soldier," the lieutenant corrected her. "Until I become a general, I'll consider myself a soldier. A soldier in an army of medics."

"You're military," repeated Yulia. "Tomorrow you'll be sent to the Arctic. Or to the Far East. Maybe even to Afghanistan. Anything can happen."

"Of course it can," he agreed, smiling with anticipation.

"Anything," echoed Yulia.

"So what?"

"Nothing. Let's talk about something else."

"No," he protested, because this subject made him happy. "Let's get it all out into the open!"

"Being in the army is like being in prison," continued Yulia, with a seriousness he had not seen in her before. "Once you've chosen it, you're in it for life. But why is that? Why not for five, or, say, ten years? What if you discover that you made the wrong decision? Does that mean you have to put up with being miserable for the rest of your life? And just go along, contributing nothing to your profession? A profession you've come to dislike, or maybe never really liked? Or not learned to do it properly because the interest isn't there? Whose idea was it to trap young people into the army, and then not let go of them until they're old? Is it like this in other countries, or only in ours? It's . . . it's . . . positively *medieval!* Diabolical!"

"I've never given it any thought," admitted Shmelev. His faith in success, his conviction that he had made the right choice were still somewhat akin to belief in the omnipotence of gold.

"Neither had I. These are my mother's thoughts. About Daddy. But now I share them."

Shmelev suddenly felt an urge to blurt out:

"I'm flying to Afghanistan. All our group's going there." But he wanted to surprise her with a letter from the battlefront even more, so he held his tongue.

"It's always like that," he said instead. "I want to talk about us, and you go on about my job."

"But that is about us," insisted Yulia, with that same, strange, adult intonation.

"I haven't kissed you for three days."

"Is that thing working?"

"What? Oh, my Grundig. I told you, didn't I, that Dad brought it from West Germany."

"Is it on?"

"You bet. I taped us just now when we were talking. As a keepsake."

He had brought the cassette with him, but it sounded somehow different here. However, Yulia's voice was still more important than the words she said.

Not surprisingly, Kabul astounded Shmelev. In the two weeks since his arrival, he had already been into the city three times—twice in APCs and once in a Gaz-69 jeep. His companions were already old hands.

He saw the center of the city, the famous "green" market, where armed Soviet soldiers strolled around with a proprietary air, poking their noses into the shops and booths.

The noise was deafening, crowds of people milled and jostled. Most of the shoppers were around the shops that sold delicious-smelling, flat, pancake-like bread. The fruit and vegetable rows were very busy, too. There were bananas, nuts, oranges, and tangerines brought from Nangarkhar province. Piles of yellowy-pink washed carrots were to be had on every side.

Shmelev was lucky—they had come to the market in the morning.

Traders set up trestle tables, covered them with woven cloths, and right there, under Shmelev's bemused gaze, set out their wares: handicrafts out of amethysts, carnelians, and lapis lazuli: necklaces, bracelets, garnet rosaries that flashed with dark red fire. They hung up carpets of all shapes and sizes, crafted with fabulous designs. Shrill-voiced striplings, brought along to assist their parents, prepared hats made of fox and wolf pelts for display—shaking them out, plumping them up, and generally making the wares look enticing. The hats seemed incredibly fluffy, reminiscent of light, golden clouds.

"Incredible!" exclaimed Shmelev over and over, turning his close-dropped head in all directions.

The market had no clearly defined limits: rows of sheepskin coats gave way to shops selling ox hides, articles knitted out of camel hair, then tea and coffee sets brought from Hong Kong, India, and China. Beyond them came the latest in television sets, digital watches to suit every taste, and superb audio equipment, boasting the world's most famous brand names.

Where else could you see something like that?

Unfortunately, death was here, too. You could easily catch a knife in your back. Or a whole shop would blow up.

Shmelev had heard about this. But like everyone else, he reacted differently to what he heard and what he saw with his own eyes. That which one sees overrides what one has heard. It's inevitable.

Shmelev sent his parents a condensed description of his visit to the market, and a more expanded one to Yulia. Both letters began and ended with the same word: "Amazing!"

In two weeks, seven letters had been sent to Kiev from Kabul: three to the parents, four to Yulia.

"I shouldn't have chosen medicine as my profession," he wrote home. "I have discovered that I am much more interested in geography and history. None of my colleagues here have even heard of what I discovered immediately. They're simply not interested. And I'm enthralled."

And he went on to relate the stories he had heard in Kabul.

"Dad!" he enthused in one letter. "Our people have built a fabulously beautiful building here in Kabul. It's the 'House of Soviet Science and Culture.' I bet that you, an architect, would be bowled over, it's that beautiful. But I was very puzzled to learn that the architect of that house is a Cypriot. Why not one of our architects?

"Kabul has existed for fifteen centuries. At first it seems disorderly, chaotic, badly planned. As for the clothes the people wear—well, you'd be hard put to imagine anything less comfortable. But that's from our point of view, of course. I was amazed to learn that an Afghan's turban can also serve as a tablecloth or a sheet, because it's fourteen meters long. Can you imagine that? You get to understand very important things here—for instance, that people don't do things without reason, just like that. I mean, they can try something, just to test the results once, but not go on repeating it for centuries. The fact that not everyone sees the reason behind things is a different matter. But I see it!"

"Taxis in Kabul are of two color combinations," he wrote on another occasion. "Black and white, and yellow and white. And do you know why?" The next eight pages were filled with a humorous account of a circumstance that could have been described easily on one page of a notebook. When Daud was in power, he ordered that all taxis should be black and white. Daud's family—and Daud himself—had very profitable connections with car spray-painting works. However, facilities were limited, and not all the taxis had been done by the time Amin took over. Among others, he rescinded Daud's instruction about the taxis. As it happens, Amin's family also had a financial interest in a painting enterprise, and had to be assured a nice profit. Yet this time, too, the order that all taxis be repainted (yellow and white) had not been fully completed by the time Amin fell and was replaced by Taraki, whose family was in a different line of business altogether.

"Mind you," Shmelev told his parents, "I don't travel around Kabul in taxis: perish the thought! We look at them out of our own BMPs."

Shmelev's parents learned a great deal about Kabul from his letters: the only thing that was missing was any mention of war. But then, he hadn't seen it yet.

Those two weeks had been unusually peaceful in Kabul.

Then came the day of departure. An armored group was heading into Pagman, and Shmelev was ordered to join it, and not waste time.

He was raring to go.

Ten minutes before departure he received a letter from home. Home! It had been brought by a friend of his father's who had been ordered to Afghanistan in connection with some construction work.

Shmelev climbed up on the armor of the BMP and opened the letter. It did not contain anything special: ". . . look after yourself, son, your mother worries constantly. So do I . . ." "Volodya, my dear son," added his mother, "be very careful. You're always so happy-go-lucky. . . . I had a dreadful nightmare . . . you were in it. . . . Of course, I know it's just my nerves. . . . I even phoned Yulia; we shed a tear together."

The armored vehicle lurched forward unexpectedly, and the letter fluttered out of Shmelev's hands into a cloud of dust.

"Never mind!" shouted a major, who had clambered up beside Shmelev.

He didn't mind: he was caught up in a new life and the journey before him. Lieutenant Shmelev of the medical corps took off toward that which one woman had sensed, and another dreamt.

◀　　◀　　◀

It didn't take him long to become accustomed to the racket of the vehicle's caterpillar tracks as it sped along. It was harder to become acclimatized to the situation and the other personnel. Of course, they were already drawing closer together into a common task, but he still felt isolated.

He was a tyro. Someone from another world, a world in which everything is different. Not long ago he had walked the streets of Kiev and gone about ordinary, everyday tasks. The last thing on his mind had been that there is war, fighting, and violence in the world. And that if for some reason they are not taking place in one area, then they are invariably present elsewhere. And can change location very quickly. Or you will change places, and find yourself in the midst of them. One should be ready for such an eventuality, of course, but how? It's not all that simple.

All the preparation he had had was a bit of training with weights in the mornings.

Much of what he'd thought and believed yesterday dissipated as he rode along. The fragments had to be gathered and rearranged into a pattern that fitted reality, but for that one had to have time. And time was not available.

Combat choppers hung over Kabul—they always had more than enough work to do. The choppers flew in pairs—never solo. That way you had four more eyes to look at the same sectors. If one of the choppers landed to carry out a mission, the other one would hover overhead, providing cover. At the same time, it would keep an eye on what was happening in the immediate vicinity on the ground. Ultimately, if one chopper had to make an emergency landing, the other would follow it down to pick up the crew before the spooks could take them prisoner.

Neither the major nor the other soldiers spared any time to look at anything but the road ahead. Shmelev, on the other hand, swiveled his head from left to right.

They had left the last of Kabul's buildings behind. The remains of some mud-brick buildings flashed by alongside the road, then the few remaining shops. Their windows were half-covered with pictures of European whores, cut out of magazines. On the left they passed the barbed-wire–encircled hospital barracks. This was where those with infectious diseases such as typhus, hepatitis, and cholera were isolated. Then the road began to wind through a gray, dusty plain that lay at the foot of the Hindu Kush. It was reminiscent of the Russian steppes, but lacked grass and the smell of flowers. This was a steppe in a fragile world.

Another twenty minutes and they entered the mountains. The mountains of war.

◄　　◄　　◄

"Yu! Now you know where I am. I'm very happy here. Kabul is surrounded by absolutely fantastic mountains. When you're among them, you can't but realize what pygmies we are. The mountains are beautiful. If only one could paint them—but they look different every day. Only a painter like Rerich could even attempt such a task. V."

◄　　◄　　◄

Before entering a tunnel the major would lift his hand, two fingers raised in a "V." That meant—are all the others vehicles there, or has someone fallen behind? The gunner would look and yell: "All there!"

The tunnels were dark and dank. The beams of the

headlights shone pink or gold inside them, or, rather, tinged with gold. That is how a heavily wounded man probably sees the sunlight reflected in a golden article on the ground beside him.

To Shmelev, the light looked golden.

The driver, Leontyev, had his head stuck out of the hatch, just in front of Shmelev. His black helmet made it look like a floating marine mine. He did not know the road's twists and turns. It would slope down steeply, and then there would be an equally steep ascent. There were stretches when the tracks of the BMP would be a mere twenty centimeters away from a sheer drop of eight hundred meters or more, if not a full kilometer.

The driver did not know the turns, but Major Obruchev had them all memorized. However, it was impossible to shout above the roar of the motor. Extending a leg wounded in a nighttime encounter with the enemy, Obruchev held on to the cannon with his right hand, and kept his left on Leontyev's helmet. He would turn the driver's head left or right, meaning that he should either slow down or speed up, and share his knowledge this way. Shmelev watched, his heart hammering.

Two other soldiers shared the armor with Shmelev. A bit behind him to the left sat rosy-cheeked Private Polenov, hanging onto his submachine gun. Every so often he would hitch up his ammunition belt as he watched the surrounding cliffs like a hawk. His gun was ready to shoot immediately. To the right, near the radio antenna, sat Private Bakhramov, as fresh-faced and rosy-cheeked as Polenov. He, too, watched the cliffs intently, and had the safety catch off his gun. At the front sat Sergeant Batyru, clutching his gun and scanning the cliffs. In a contest as to who had the rosiest cheeks, the sergeant would have been streets ahead of the others. Together and individually they were doing their duty. Their eyes searched the rocks, because an ambush could occur anywhere, at any moment. They were ready for battle. Their combat-readiness had long become a conditioned reflex here in Afghanistan, and distinguished them from those who had not yet acquired it. And from the people they had been in their own first months of service.

The motor suddenly gave out in a narrow, dark ravine. They stopped. Without a word, all the soldiers raised the cold, short barrels of their guns. The vehicle traveling behind them pulled up too, as there was no room to pass. To their left the cliff fell away in a steep drop, to their right it sheared up into the sky. They were in a very vulnerable spot. Although they could give heavy return fire, they couldn't get away. Not far away the charred remains of an APC stuck out of the yellow water of a mountain stream. Farther on they could see a wrecked bus and a destroyed tank. Shmelev would have never believed that a tank could be so badly damaged.

Major Obruchev and the driver, Leontyev, started trying to make quick repairs. Raising the hood, they delved into the hot, oily entrails of the BMP.

The soldiers quickly divided the surrounding cliffs into quadrants, each one watching only his assigned sector. Experience counted for nothing here—the only indications of danger were movement or sound. Either of these can be noted equally well by old hands and newcomers.

The only difference is that the new boy may not immediately believe his eyes or his ears, and decide to check again, just to be sure. That is a fatal mistake. An experienced soldier won't wait, because he knows that the speed of reaction is what counts in the mountains. Either the enemy gets you, or you get him first.

Far away, up ahead, a couple of helicopters crossed the blue of the sky. Shmelev watched them, and saw white puffs of smoke—traces of Oerlikon missiles fired by the spooks from some mountain fastness at the choppers.

"Swiss manufacture," observed the sergeant.

Shmelev stared at the rocks surrounding them. Each one of us, he realized finally, could be shot at from that rock over there. He stared at the rock intently, but a moment later it would seem that a shot would come from behind another one. And he would transfer his stare to it.

This went on for quite a long time. Danger was everywhere. And slowly but surely, he began to change. He felt real fear for his life, and then shook it off. After that he no longer felt isolated, but one of the team.

Probably the only way to determine the unity of men in war is under threat of imminent Death.

If only they could get under way! But things did not look at all promising. The major limped over to the second vehicle. A senior lieutenant jumped down off its armor and strode toward the major. They discussed something for a few minutes, and then decided to try to push-start the first vehicle, with the second one doing the pushing. Leontyev, smeared with grease from head to foot, slammed down the wide green hood and climbed back to his levers and pedals. The major hoisted himself back onto the armor.

"Hold tight!" he shouted.

With a roar, the second vehicle advanced on them, and they almost fell off, so hard was the impact of many tons of metal. The armor under the clinging men seemed to leap and buckle, but then settled back as they moved forward. The motor fired, "caught," and snarled back into life. A cloud of choking black smoke spewed out of the exhaust and washed over Shmelev in a searing wave.

"Come on, come on," he muttered. "At least we're moving again!"

Leontyev managed to get up a speed of sixty kilometers per hour on a straight stretch of road. A concrete bridge appeared some forty meters ahead. The major suddenly jerked as if stung, and wrenched Leontyev's head around so hard that he almost broke his neck.

"Turn right!" he yelled at the top of his voice. "Right!"

Leontyev obeyed unquestioningly, sending the heavy vehicle down an incline. Everyone held on for dear life. Only when they reached the bottom of the dried-out gulch spanned by the bridge did they see what the major had spotted: the first span of the bridge had been blown up. It must have been done not long ago, because there were no tracks to indicate any traffic bypassing the now useless structure. Their tracks were the first.

"Yu! Moonlight in Kabul is a relic of former centuries. Curfew belongs to our time only. Everything here is so jumbled. Helicopters share the sky with mosque domes. The streets are cluttered with wooden carts ('karachis') carrying firewood, camels, Toyotas, Mercedes, and also Zhigulis and Volgas. Women walk along the footpaths with green and black nets over their faces, past our tanks, APCs, and armed soldiers. It's incredible! Strange that I might never have seen all this. It sounds silly, but I owe it all to the war. I'm keeping my eyes peeled. V."

Toward evening they reached the position of a motorized artillery battalion. After the racket and dust of the journey the voices of the artillerymen, the howling of the wind, and the frenzied barking of two ferocious dogs seemed quiet and dull, as if heard through a thick quilt.

The major heard the battalion commander's report and checked the camouflage. Then he asked after someone.

"He's in the hospital," answered the commander.

"For preservation," quipped Shmelev.

Everyone laughed, but the commander explained further:

"Tonsils."

The newly arrived soldiers trooped off to wash. There were no rosy cheeks visible now: all faces were covered with a thick layer of white dust. A good kilo of it had settled into the creases of their battle jackets. The major looked like a miller after a busy day. The artillerymen, however, looked as spruce as the newcomers had been at the start of their trek. Each one wore a bulletproof vest, with ammunition belts slung across flat stomachs.

A busy road ran at the foot of the plateau on which the artillerymen were encamped, and it was their job to guard it. There was an Afghan government army post on one side of the valley, and a Soviet one on the opposite side. The situation along the road was tense.

"The spooks tried twice today," said the commander. "But open attacks are not really a problem any-more."

"What is?" asked the major.

"Mines. We're fair worn out locating them."

The road, a sector of which could be seen from the plateau, linked the north and the south of the country. There were no other roads, just this one. Its condition was appalling: trucks carrying fuel and mineral fertilizers, military traffic, and civilian buses all lurched, bumped, creaked, and broke down on ruts and holes left by mines.

"It's not hard to imagine what would happen if even one sector of this road were to become impassable," remarked the major.

The encampment was surrounded by defenses: on three sides there was a circumvallation of linked trenches. Not far from the edge of the cliff there was a massive stone building. Something like headquarters. On the northern edge of the camp Shmelev spotted an ornate latrine, constructed out of green ammunition boxes, identical to the ones they had brought with them. Barrels filled with sand stood around everywhere, to offer cover from bullets and shell fragments.

The evening had a magical quality about it. Faint rosy streaks chased across the deep enamel of the sky as the sun sank behind the mountains of Iran.

Bang! Rat-tat-tat-tat-tat! A lengthy machine-gun volley drowned out thoughts of anything else. The men scattered to battle stations. A dry, strong detonation shook the ground beside Shmelev, who stood on one spot as if turned to stone. A flare shot into the sky, and hung there on its parachute.

The major hurried through the grenade launchers' trench.

The machine gunners reached their stations first, and set to work immediately, weaving a web of tracer bullets above the valley.

"To the left—one hundred!" shouted someone. "To the left—one hundred!" The light of the tracers exposed targets. The cannon of the two BMPs joined in, drowning out all other sound. The intensity of the fire was stupefying: it seemed that the shells from the BMPs hit a steep, far-off slope almost as soon as they left the barrels of the cannons.

Shmelev's initial fear receded. He began to wonder why there seemed to be no return fire from the spooks.

A tall, incredibly thin man appeared from behind a BMP lugging a huge movie camera. "How the hell did he get here?" thought Shmelev. In the meantime, the man leaped with his camera into the gunners' trench, and started filming their tense faces and the barrels of their guns. Then he lay on his back and aimed his camera at the fiery traces of the shells from the BMPs.

"They're making a film!" realized Shmelev. "They're doing all this for a film! Good Lord, when there's danger, I want to laugh, and when it's funny—like now—I get scared stiff. I've still got a lot to learn out here!"

The business finished just as abruptly as it had begun. The dust settled and gunsmoke drifted over toward the tanks, which were surrounded by walls of round stones. The cameraman, plus two men dressed in paratroopers' gear and red knitted caps, headed for the kitchen, accompanied by a couple of officers.

Late dusk enveloped the plateau.

"You work like a dog all day," Shmelev heard one soldier grumble to another as they washed, "and then those bloody film people want you to stage a battle just like the real thing."

"Still, your face will be on the silver screen," replied the other, laughing loudly. "Your girl will see it, and maybe take her undies off when you come back, eh?"

"Dear Yulia! I've said good-bye to Kabul. Must rush, and get a place on the armor. We're pulling out. Volodya."

In the morning they began the last leg of their journey. The convoy was the same, but there was a new BMP out in front. There was nobody riding on its armor; it only carried a crew.

The road ran south. The sun shone brightly over the valley. As was his wont, Shmelev studied the countryside with interest. He was falling in love with this beautiful country. From time to time he would raise his field glasses to his eyes. Whenever a lone bird swept across the sky, he would follow its flight until it disappeared over the horizon.

Then the leading vehicle gave a sudden lurch, and became enveloped in a sheet of transparent flame. A gout of black smoke obscured the turret, and the blazing vehicle was rocked by two heavy, dull explosions. It stopped dead.

Shmelev's vehicle braked sharply.

"Mines!" cried the major, jumping down and running toward the burning BMP. Everyone else scrambled down after him.

Shmelev grabbed his medical kit, prepared for something unknown. At that moment, a man clambered out of the flames. He was smothered in blood and ash. Rolling down to the ground, he writhed around on one spot. His left hand was smashed, and sharp fragments stuck out of the sleeve of his battle jacket. Shmelev sprinted over, and tried to make him stop moving. He saw at a glance that the hand was beyond saving, but gangrene could be averted. He pulled out his bayonet, and chopped off the hand then and there. As he struggled to apply a tourniquet, he saw another soldier writhing on the beside him. He, too, had managed to claw his way out of the BMP, despite horrific injuries to his legs. Shmelev dropped the tourniquet and devoted his energies to helping the second soldier. He didn't yell, but made ghastly moaning noises, showing the whites of his eyes.

Shmelev could see that both legs had been completely shattered: there couldn't be a whole bone left in them. Here, too, was the threat of gangrene.

He pressed the soldier bodily to the ground, and began to do what had to be done. The soldiers gasped and gulped lungfuls of hot Afghan wind, and Shmelev labored on. Smoke, heat, and sweat stung his face. A fearful task. Bloody. Hellish. But Shmelev was strong. He had never felt so strong in his life. He pressed the soldier down with his body and kept working.

His task possessed every fiber of his being.

Having finished with one leg, he started on the second, oblivious of the shouts, flames, and roar of motors around him.

By the time the amputation was finished, the BMP driver had managed to get out of the burning vehicle. His face was covered in blood, and his hair was singed into a matted mess. But he stayed on his feet, issued orders, and suggested something about the damaged turret.

The driver had, in fact, suffered no serious injury—slight burns and a touch of concussion, that was all. The blood on his face was that of the gunner, who had been killed beside him. But Shmelev, gripped by amputation frenzy, could no longer think straight. He came face-to-face with the driver.

All he saw were the driver's dilated eyes and the blood trickling off his chin. Drawing a deep breath, Shmelev raised his bayonet.

The driver backed away in alarm.

But the lieutenant was quick on his feet.

He seized the driver's head in a vicelike grip, and brought his bayonet down to the driver's throat.

He wanted to amputate the driver's head! Everyone around them froze in horror and disbelief.

"Break!" yelled the major. "Stop! Back! Quick!"

He threw himself on Shmelev, but there seemed to be no force strong enough to pull the lieutenant away from his victim. The soldiers, recovering from their stupefaction, knocked Shmelev and the driver to the ground, bestraddled them, and wrenched the bayonet out of Shmelev's hands.

Shmelev suddenly started to laugh, bared his teeth, and sawed at the empty air with his hand. "Now, now," he repeated. "Now, now . . ." and made sawing motions.

The soldiers held him down as he sawed.

Twenty minutes later the helicopter that had been summoned to their assistance took them on board and swept up into the sky.

◄   ◄   ◄

The surgeon who examined both wounded soldiers in the hospital affirmed that the amputations carried out by Shmelev had been necessary.

Passing by the psychiatric wing he added: "Pity that it had to end like that. A great pity. Although hope, as the ancients used to say, exists even at the brink of the grave."

◄   ◄   ◄

Vladimir Shmelev, former junior lieutenant of the Limited Contingent of Soviet Forces in Afghanistan, lay on a narrow bunk in a straitjacket, his back to the world, staring at the wall. Possibly he was thinking about that wall.

Finale

On 15 May 1988 I was riding the armor of the commander's vehicle, on the way back from Jellalabad to Kabul. Colonel Yuri Starov's APC led a column of 310 tanks, tractors, infantry-fighting vehicles, and APCs. This was the first "Geneva" column. There was not a news agency in the world that did not report on this event.

Could it really be the end of the war?

As the column moved off it was controlled by ten UN observers. We arrived together. The planes flew without lights both inside and out. We landed with the help of aerial illumination flares. Before dawn, the area of the column's position was shelled by several dozen rockets. Despite the shelling, a sleepless night, and the rush of preparation, everyone was in top form. Officers and soldiers radiated a glow like a well-oiled gun.

Homeward bound! When a war finishes, not everyone rejoices.

Those whose careers were built on the war experience regret.

Those who dealt in weapons and money on the black market are desolated.

Those who sent and peddled hundreds of kilos of drugs to the Soviet Union, panic.

But still, the majority rejoice. The column stretched for several kilometers. We moved forward under the protective fire of multibarrel rocket launchers. Military choppers assured protection from the air. Home, home, to our own land . . .

We passed alien, ruined villages—dilapidated shops, broken planks of useless gates, mud-brick houses reduced to rubble.

Will life ever return here? And if it does—when?

We drove past former rice fields, which had turned into stinking marshes.

Past former sugarcane fields, surrounded now by barbed wire and warning signs in Russian: "MINES."

Past one-time gardens, reduced now to black, charred stumps, the haunt of revolting, waiting vultures.

Past a river that had once been clear and beautiful, marred now by disabled APCs sticking out of its muddy waters, its banks churned up by so many APC tracks, defiled by oil and fire.

Past, past, past.

I sat on the armor and looked ahead.

It was necessary to think about all these terrible things. It was necessary to think about my young fellow countrymen who had met untimely deaths in this land. About the million Afghans who had lost their lives. About this abused and disfigured country. About those who had survived, and would now be returning to their homes. About this ghastly war, which, though officially ended, has not been left behind, but returns home with the soldiers, in their hearts and souls, riding on their shoulders. About human stupidity and human fate. About the consequences of this war for the world and for our two countries. And about much more in that vein.

But all I could think about was trivia. Tanks clanked, choppers clattered overhead, artillery boomed, and I thought about trifles. I thought that this was probably the first war ever in the course of whose nine years nobody ever heard a love story. A love story involving a foreign soldier and a local beauty. There was not one single such instance, which gives a human dimension to any war. Even the worst war imaginable.

This war could not boast of any spark of warmth or humanity. Not a single ray of light.

After a ten-hour march, the column reached Kabul without any casualties. In another five to seven hours, after rest and a meeting, it was due to move again, to the state border of the USSR.

As for me, I had been ordered by my editor to carry out an urgent assignment: to interview leading Afghan personalities. I was to note down their views on the future of the revolutionary changes in Afghanistan, and record the steadfastness and optimism of its people.

. . . Late that evening I arrived at a villa occupied by a Soviet friend. Having washed off a pall of white dust, I got down to work.

The study in which I worked on my interviews was on the ground floor of the villa. My friend went to bed on the first floor, having taken the precaution of placing a loaded machine gun on a prayer mat beside his bed, and a pistol under his pillow.

I thought I would be finished by five or six o'clock in the morning. Then I would check through what I'd written one last time, and relay it to Moscow by phone. At around eight-thirty I would be free to leave.

Two explosions went off simultaneously.

Ground-to-ground missiles.

The next couple of rockets came closer: glass vibrated in the windows, and the dogs began to howl. Rocket fire, as always, got the machine guns going. There seemed to be no order to the firing; it was scattered far and wide. I did my best to concentrate on my work, but the loud chatter of machine guns interrupted even the most familiar, standard revolutionary phrases.

I put aside my pen and got up. The blinds were not solid, and I realized that all this time I would have made a perfect target for anyone outside.

I switched off the light as a safety measure, but how on earth could I write? So I pressed the switch again.

The shooting didn't stop. I swept my papers off the table, took my notebook, and retreated to the lavatory. In this safe bolt hole I switched on the light, locked the door, and settled down on a toilet made by some firm called Admiral. I rested my notebook on my knees, placed a piece of paper on it, and continued an interrupted sentence: "... only our faith in revolutionary ideals ..."

Meanwhile, the shooting continued unabated. Now, however, it sounded muffled. When rocket missiles exploded, the lavatory door would shudder slightly on its hinges. I was not worried, and went on writing. The light was bright; I wrote quickly and easily. My only complaint was that my back felt very stiff. Still, I knew that nobody was training the sights of his gun on me, and I was not at risk.

Every time I covered a sheet of paper, I would lay it on the floor by my right foot.

From time to time I would go back and reread an earlier page, and then continue. The pile of sheets covered with handwriting grew. The shooting had stopped long ago. The silence was shattered by the cry of a muezzin from behind the wall of the neighboring villa: he was calling the faithful to the first prayer of the day.

That meant it must be 5:00 .A.M.

The job was done.

I saluted, flushed the basin three times, and walked out of the toilet.

◂ ◂ ◂

"I could never shake off a feeling of depression in Afghanistan. I felt it most sharply even before I flew to Kabul, at the moment when, sitting in my apartment in Moscow with friends on New Year's Eve, I heard about the Soviet government's decision to send troops into Afghanistan. It seemed to me then that I saw a dark tunnel into which my country was plunging, I felt as though I were choking—not at all typical of me. But the most amazing thing is that this reaction was shared by the vast majority of Soviet citizens. Of course, it changed nothing: official approbation endowed the fateful step with a sort of triumphal rectitude. And so it was during all those years of the war, the longest waged by Russia since 1813: the people lived in grief, and officialdom basked in the glory of doctrine."

(Extract from an interview given by the author to the CBS television network.)

Index

INDEX

INDEX

INDEX

Order, maintenance of, 54
Orlov (Political Officer), 121–22

Pain, struggle with, 96–97
Pakistan, border incident, 67–83
Paratroopers, 145–46
Party functionaries, as officials, 54
Peasants, and revolutionary
    government, 57
People's Democratic Party of
    Afghanistan (PDPA), 5
Personal experience, 12–13
Personal integrity of journalists, 56
Polenov (Private), 163
Political figures, moral sickness of,
    101
Political indoctrination of soldiers,
    121–22
Popular music, soldiers' views, 119–
    20
Posttraumatic stress syndrome, 97–
    99
Prisoners taken by guerrillas, 141
Propaganda for Afghan war, 51–63,
    121–22
Psychiatric disorders, 172–73
Psychiatric hospital, military, 97–99
"Psychos" in armed services, 117
Pushtu refugees, view of war, 133–
    36
Puzanov (Soviet ambassador), 5

Qualities, human, war and, 97

Rashidov (Private), 68–71, 73
Reactions to war's end, 177
Recruits, 24–27
Red Army, Military Code, 77
Refugees, view of war, 133–36
Request for Soviet intervention, 55,
    136
Responsibility for actions, of
    soldiers, 67–83
Reversed binoculars principle, 53–
    54
Revolution, 50–51
Revolutionary government,
    Afghanistan, 57–58
  Soviet control, 59–62

Roads, 168
Rost, Victor, 119, 123–24, 128–29
Rumors, 7
Rusakov, Sergei, "Kobzon," 120–
    21, 128–29
Russian people, and Afghan war,
    30

SAM-7, missiles, 145–46
Schools
  Afghan, coeducation in, 57
  Russian, lessons in manliness,
    113
Serikov (Lieutenant Colonel), 140,
    144
Shmelev, Vladimir, 151–73
Sikander (staff interpreter), 35–36, 41
Singer, popular, in Afghanistan, 89–
    92
Smertenyuk (Private), 140, 144
Smirnov (Lieutenant), letter from,
    113–15
Social change, 50–51
Sokol, Galina, 89, 93
Soldiers
  battle experiences, 19–46, 107–
    29, 151–73
  burial of, 25, 125–27
  involvement of, propaganda, 55
  responsibility for actions, 67–83
  views of war, 8–9
    understanding, 33–34, 136–38
Soviet Gosteleradio, 58
Soviet Komsomol, advisers in
    Kabul, 61
Soviet Union
  ambassadors to Afghanistan, 5–6,
    53–54
  army commanders, 142
  Communist Party members in
    Kabul, 7
  control of revolutionary
    government, 59–62
  forces in Afghanistan, 5, 7–9
  intervention in Afghanistan,
    request for, 55, 136
  moral sickness of leaders, 101
  Red Army Military Code, 77
  See also Afghanistan war

186

INDEX

About the Author

SOVIET JOURNALIST GENNADY BOCHAROV first arrived in Kabul in February 1980, one month after Soviet troops entered Afghanistan. Over the next eight years he returned regularly, reporting candidly from the front. His articles showed a consistent disregard for official recommendations and were celebrated as among the few sources of genuine information about the Afghanistan war. Mr. Bocharov's books have sold over one and a half million copies in the USSR. He is a regular correspondent for one of the most popular Soviet weeklies, *Literaturnaya Gazeta,* and is known for his investigative writing on the Soviet space program, the military, and the civil aviation authorities; natural disasters such as the Armenian earthquake; interviews with literary and political figures; and reports from the front lines of wars all over the world. He lives in Moscow.